Building Extreme PCs

Building Extreme PCs
Ben Hardwidge

The complete guide to computer modding

O'REILLY®

First edition for the United States, its territories and dependencies,
Central and South America, and Canada published in 2006 by O'Reilly Media, Inc.

O'Reilly Media, Inc.
1005 Gravenstein Highway North
Sebastopol, CA 95472
USA
www.oreilly.com

Editorial Director: John Neidhart, O'Reilly Media

The O'Reilly logo is a registered trademark of O'Reilly Media, Inc.

O'Reilly books may be purchased for educational, business, or sales promotional use.
For more information, contact our corporate/institutional sales department:
(800) 998-9938 or corporate@oreilly.com

International Standard Book No. 0-596-10136-8

This book was conceived by:
ILEX, Cambridge, England
www.ilex-press.com

ILEX Editorial, Lewes:
Publisher: Alastair Campbell
Managing Director: Stephen Paul
Creative Director: Peter Bridgewater
Managing Editor: Tom Mugridge
Editor: Ben Renow-Clarke
Art Director: Julie Weir
Designer: Jon Raimes
Design Assistant: Kate Haynes

ILEX Research, Cambridge:
Development Art Director: Graham Davis
Technical Art Director: Nicholas Rowland

Printed and bound in China

9 8 7 6 5 4 3 2 1

Contents

Over the last five years, a new type of PC user has started to spread across the globe. Starting off as a small group of specialist über-geeks, this new breed has now all but taken over the top end of the PC industry. Take a walk past the computer stores, and you'll see windows stacked with PC cases with windowed side panels, enough cold cathode lights to illuminate a Vegas nightclub, and heatsinks and fans more reminiscent of street racing components than PC system parts.

Now a mainstream hobby, PC enthusiasm is bolstered by a hard core of people who (sometimes) love fast PCs more than they love life itself. These are the people that their friends and family repeatedly call for free technical support; the people who would rather spend a week in a darkened room fiddling with components and cabling than lazing on a beach in Bermuda.

These are the guys that see the PC as the most flexible toy you can imagine. A toy that can do infinitely more than word processing or e-mail, and one that's crying out to be pushed to its limits whatever the consequences. This is a scene where buyers have little (if any) respect for the warranties that come with components; they just want to see what they're really capable of, and build a PC that will be the envy of all their friends.

This scene is also a rebellion against the uninspired and restricted PC designs that we've been forced to tolerate for decades. In the PC enthusiast scene, bland and boring computers in beige cases are about as welcome as Eminem at a Republican Party fund raiser. This is a world where PCs are filled with colored tubes for their water-cooling systems, where components run at speeds unheard of in PC World, and where it's not uncommon to find a computer built into a kitchen appliance, or even a cuddly toy.

This book is an introduction to that world, gathering together the very best PCs that have been produced by the scene, as well as giving you all the basic tips and tricks that you'll need to have a go at it yourself. If you've ever fancied trying to build your own PC from scratch, or even tweaking the one that you've already got, then this is the best place to start.

If you were expecting a full-on technical guide to the scary depths of PCs—in-depth tutorials on constructing your own phase change cooler, perhaps, or building a PC into an amoeba—then you may not find what you're looking for. However, we will cover all of the most important aspects of PC modding and customization, with tips that won't become obsolete in the days between this being written and you reading it—something that is always a factor in this fast-moving world.

Requiring a unique combination of craftsmanship, technical knowledge, and creativity, PCs are today's ultimate hobby. Whether you want to find out how to overclock your PC, silence its noisy fans, or just find out what might be possible, read on.

Introduction

010 > 011

Where it all began

> Back in the 1970s, the future of the home computer was all in the hands of a few visionaries and eccentrics.

The eerie lights and flashing LCD displays associated with the PC modding and customization movement might be a new phenomenon, but the idea of building and customizing your own PC is as old as the home computer itself.

Back in the 1970s, the idea of what a computer should look like, or even what it did, was far less defined than it is now. With no hardware standards to adhere to and no pre-installed operating system to run, the future of the home computer was all in the hands of a few visionaries and eccentrics—men such as Apple's Steve Jobs or Commodore's Jack Tramiel—and they often released their computers in kit form.

It didn't matter that these "computers" were often about as useful as non-stick Scotch tape; it was the fact that you could build your own that counted. This instantly appealed to the same strange part of the mind that thinks spending a whole month painting the correct insignia onto a model of Star Trek's U.S.S. Enterprise is a productive use of time, except building your own computer was more like tinkering with the unknown.

Examples of these first customizable computers included the first Apple computer, which came as a piece of circuit board that hobbyists would have to connect their own display and keyboard to. Then came Sinclair's build-your-own digital watch kit and its MK14 (microcomputer kit 14) in the late '70s; a kit that still managed to look like a kit even after it had been built. A few years later you could still save yourself some money on a ZX81 or the classic rubber-keyed ZX Spectrum if you were prepared to build it in kit form. In fact, you can still buy yourself a ZX81 kit (from www.zx81kit.co.uk) if you so desire!

Basically, if you were looking for a challenging introvert hobby that didn't involve going outside, but instead gave you something that you could spend hours proudly admiring and then fiddling about with, then this was far more satisfying than gluing together a model Saturn rocket or messing around in the shed trying to build a shelf; this was a taste of the future. Not only that, you could also upgrade them by installing—hush—more memory or—gasp—a joystick interface!

If you didn't like your chances of putting together a working computer (most didn't), you could still buy a ready-built one, get it home, and then program in your own games and applications. Magazines suddenly sprang up whose sole purpose was to provide you with pages and pages of BASIC code to type into your computer. After several days of typing, you might just be able to recreate a poor rendition of Pong, or in some cases, just a simple animated graphic.

The home computer hobby was now big business, but this was only the beginning. By 1981, IBM had already started producing what we now know as the PC, but it was far from the customizable box of any shape and size that we know today. Based on a 4.77MHz Intel 8088 processor, with 64KB of RAM and no graphical capabilities (yes, the first PCs were text-only), the IBM PC 5150 wasn't only dull to use—it was astonishingly dull to look at.

We can allow for changes in taste and fashion, but seeing as the first dinky Apple Macintosh and the minimally stylish ZX Spectrum were floating around in 1983, it's safe to say that the IBM PC never looked good. In fact, it's amazing that the PC became the dominant force it is today when you looked at it then. How could this be the computer that would transform our lives in the next 20 years?

Right: **Hobbyists had to add their own case, keyboard, and monitor to the circuit board supplied with an Apple1 kit.**

Above: **The very first PC wasn't much to look at. It's difficult to believe that this would be the computer that would take over our lives 20 years later.**

Right: **Sinclair's MK14 still managed to look like a kit after it had been built.**

Far right: **Sinclair's computers often had a cheaper DIY kit option for the brave and the stupidly optimistic, such as this ZX81 kit.**

From Science of Cambridge: the new MK 14.
Simplest, most advanced, most flexible
microcomputer – in kit form.

only
£39.95
(+ 8% VAT)

Science of
CAMBRIDGE

Thanks to Juan Villa and Tix from www.1000bit.net for the ZX81 photography

012 > 013

Where it all began 2

> It was IBM opening up its standard that made the PC the dominant success it is today.

The reason why the PC took off is simple, and it's all down to IBM opening up its PC hardware standard. This meant that anyone else was welcome to use it and produce a "PC compatible" computer, which seemed to contemporaries like an incredibly foolish idea. Hermann Hauser, the former head of Acorn Computers, told me that "at the time we thought this made no sense—it's clearly a competitive market and we should hog the technology rather than license it." In retrospect, however, he had to say that "with hindsight we should have had a marketing strategy—it was IBM opening up its standard that made the PC the dominant success it is today."

Whatever IBM's reasoning, opening up the PC standard made a huge impact. Other companies could build a home computer that could do anything, whether it was playing the latest games or processing your small business' accounts. Companies such as Amstrad saw an opportunity to cash in by manufacturing affordable PC-compatible computers like the PC1512 and PC1640. These basic IBM-compatible systems offered all the basics for PC games and business-use for as little as $750. Compaq and Dell ran with the same idea.

The only problem with these PCs was, as the eighties drew to a close, their four-color CGA graphics, huge 5.25in floppy drives, and pitiful, bleepy PC speakers made them look laughable next to the Commodore Amiga and Atari ST when it came to games. This would be fine if they were customizable like today's PCs, but they weren't. You could perform small upgrades to the memory, and you normally had a couple of 8-bit expansion slots, but beyond that you were looking at a whole new PC.

The problem was that while all of these PCs may have conformed to the same hardware standard in terms of basic specifications, there was nothing to lay down the law in terms of what size and shape it had to be. You couldn't just buy a new motherboard for your PC; it wouldn't fit unless you were prepared to hack it up, so instead you had to buy everything again. This was soon to end, though, with the advent of the IBM AT standard and the Intel 80286 series of processors.

The idea behind the AT standard was that every motherboard would be roughly the same size and shape, have its keyboard port (the same as the IBM AT keyboard port, from where it gets its name) in the same place, and would also use the same power connectors and power supply requirements. As a result, you could theoretically install any AT motherboard inside any AT case. If you were wise enough to buy one of these, then you could gradually upgrade your PC as time went on, taking it all the way from a 16MHz 386 to a 450MHz Pentium II, replacing the motherboard as you needed.

Corporations like IBM, Compaq, and Dell ignored the standard at this time and continued to produce proprietary PC designs, but a growing group of home users jumped on the idea and started building the PCs that they wanted to build. Now you could build a PC exactly to your spec, with the precise components and software you wanted as well. Not only that, but you'd learn a few tricks while you were doing it. Later on, the ATX standard followed, offering the ability to shutdown the computer through software, larger motherboards, and a port bracket that accommodated far more than a simple keyboard port. The stage was set for the homemade PC industry to grow even larger.

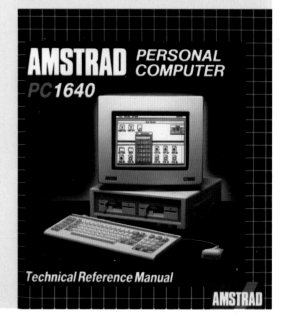

Left: **Now that all motherboards conform to standards, you can fit a motherboard like this into just about any full-size ATX case.** Right: **The manual for Amstrad's PC1640, which was one of the first IBM-compatible PCs to be affordable enough for home use.**

Left: **The AT standard meant that you could upgrade your PC all the way from a 386 that took 5.25in floppy disks to a 450MHz Pentium II with a CD burner.**
Below: **The PC found it hard to be taken seriously early on when its games looked like this.**

Razor - lead singer for the punk band,
"Razor and the Scummettes."

START

014 > 015

Beyond the DIY system

> Computer hobbyists wanted to show off their technical knowledge beyond the ability to install a motherboard.

By the 1990s, the concept of the "build your own PC" was widespread, including everyone from students showing off their technical prowess, to dads looking for a new hobby. However, at this time, home-built PCs looked the same as the PCs you bought from the shops. With the same beige towers, the same predictable insides, and—more often than not—a similar price, the DIY PC needed to evolve if it wanted to become a real hobby.

It just wasn't enough to build a PC and be done with it; computer hobbyists wanted to put an elitist personal stamp on their PC that showed off their exclusive technical knowledge and expertise beyond the ability to install a motherboard. Thankfully, a godsend arrived with the post 486-generation of processors, and it was called overclocking (see page 108).

We'll go into more detail on overclocking later on, but these early enthusiasts discovered ways of running a processor beyond its basic speed by using system clock settings designed for a faster processor. By forcing your 90MHz processor to run at 120MHz, you could get an extra 30MHz of speed for free.

It didn't take long for a whole industry to spring up around overclocking, producing powerful cooling devices to help you overclock your PC even further. These started simple—larger heatsinks and bigger fans—but soon evolved into water-cooling kits and even refrigeration systems. It didn't take long before people caught on to the fact that these kinds of cooling systems could also be made desirable by making them look cool. Soon, hundreds of wild and wacky heatsink designs sprang up (not all of which were actually any good at cooling).

Computer hardware junkies loved all of this, but they also wanted to show off their components, not to mention their system building skills, and people started modifying their cases (a term that later evolved into "modding") to include windowed side panels so that you could see the insides. This practice became so huge that now, many cases actually come with the option of pre-modded side panels.

The most famous modding tool is the Dremel (see page 86). You may be familiar with the TV advertisements in which you're told all the household jobs it can do, but while the Dremel can cut, sand, and polish household items, it can also do the same for PC cases. It's not just cases that people mod either. In fact, altering any component, whether it's replacing the cooler from a graphics card with a quieter one or etching a design into your case, it's all a form of modding.

All of this has now led to the ultimate form of modding, which is abandoning the shop-bought case completely and building your own instead. You can see a range of great modding projects at the back of this book, demonstrating that you can not only build your own case, but you can pretty much mod anything you want to into a PC.

The final piece of this puzzle came about in 2002 when VIA launched its Mini-ITX EPIA motherboard platform. It's a new standard of motherboard that measures just 170 x 170mm, with everything integrated into the motherboard, including the CPU, graphics, sound, and networking. All you have to add is memory and a power supply—and an external 55W power brick is all you need to power it, too.

All of this made it ideal for modding projects. EPIA boards aren't particularly powerful, so they can't be used for 3D games, but this in turn makes their cooling requirements minimal, meaning that they can be safely shoehorned into just about anything. You can see a whole gallery of the hundreds of Mini-ITX projects that have been completed at www.mini-itx.com.

Far left: **Modern cases such as Thermaltake's Tsunami even come with their sides "pre-modded" with windows.**
Left: **You polish; Dremel polishes. You sand; Dremel sands. You hack up teddy bear to make into PC; Dremel loves that too.**

Right: **VIA's tiny Mini-ITX** motherboards are not only affordable, but you can also squeeze them into just about anything...
Below: **Mini-ITX projects** include everything from teddy bears to retro computers, kitchen appliances to model cars

016 > 017

PC enthusiasm today

> Every day, logs are updated with home-built PCs and outrageous designs that range from the awe-inspiring to the slightly disappointing.

After breaking out from the barriers of obscurity, PC enthusiasm is now a thriving mainstream hobby that has spawned hundreds of technology websites, stacks of magazines across the world, and regular meetings with fellow enthusiasts. In fact, one PC modding magazine's circulation went up by 19% in the space of just six months in 2004, which shows just how quickly PC enthusiasm is growing as a hobby.

You only need to check out the "Project Logs" section of the forums at www.bit-tech.net to see just how huge the worldwide modding scene is. Every day, more and more updates appear that detail home-built PCs and outrageous designs that range from the awe-inspiring to the slightly disappointing. Either way, it's always heart-warming to see the responses from the modding community on the site. These are never anything but encouraging, and usually come with tips and tricks on how other modders would improve things. And that's just one example; there are plenty of other sites dedicated to modding and PC customization as well, such as Corsair's "Case mod of the month" competition (see www.corsairmemory.com/corsair/community/case_mod_month.html).

PC enthusiasts no longer have to trawl through obscure Taiwanese websites to find the elusive components they're after. They're all readily available online, and in many cases, even in local stores. Even big stores like PC World or CompUSA have their own high-end enthusiasts' section, and sponsor modding events.

While the PC was previously seen as just a business machine that could also play games, it's now viewed by many as the ultimate gaming machine. In fact, it's not uncommon for people to spend two grand on a PC just to play the latest games—helped by the fact that many of the people involved in the scene are big kids with a huge disposable income.

A pretty fair indicator that something has become a hit is when it starts to get taken seriously by big business, and every major player in the PC market has been quick to capitalize on the PC enthusiast scene. Intel has its monstrously expensive Pentium Extreme Edition; AMD has its similarly pricey, but well specced Athlon 64 FX; and NVIDIA has recently launched its SLI technology, enabling you to run two top-end graphics cards at the same time. Even Dell produces XPS PCs and laptops aimed at the technology enthusiast market.

This phenomenon is continuing to expand, with more and more products appearing all the time. The chances are that there's at least one PC enthusiast in every circle of friends somewhere, and in some cases (note the "some") it's now even socially acceptable to start a techie conversation about PCs at your local bar.

Left: **You know something's a hit when Dell jumps on the bandwagon.**

Myst IV ® Revelation

April 2005: Dutch Modder Robert Stoppel's Aquarium Mod

Here's a triumph of design and vision: a mod that's also a functioning aquarium. We kid you not: this PC is fully surrounded with water and is connected to outside world through 4 glass cylinders. Cables, connectors and fresh cold air are sent from the furniture to the PC through these tubes. And we think the Neon Tetras are a great touch!

March 2005: DOOM3 Honored in a Mod
Legendary Modder Paul Capello Captures the Essence of the Game

No doubt this year will see a lot of mods on a DOOM3 theme. But we wager few will surpass this entry from one of our favorite modders, Paul Capello. With his background in carpentry and crafts and his extreme attention to detail, Paul always turns in a mod to make us stand up and take notice. Paul's won several of our Mod of the Month awards. And he's featured in an interview in our March issue of Currents.

Sheldog23
Multimodder

Join Date: Jan 2004
Location: Austin, TX
Posts: 166

OK, another update. Heheh. If you can't tell I have been putting this off. Been so [busy?] lately. Home, work, website, new Austin Modders stuff, Prep for the April LAN. it's [...] by the end of the day I wouldn't feel like adding a worklog. I finally got so far that [...] do it. so without further ado..

The Top
We went through several designs for the top. A lot of them were your standard wi[...] up using a design that was originally going to be on the front but we thought it wa[...]

Here it is with the fans in and with lights out.

018 > 019

But why?

> Designing and building your own PC taps the creative part of your brain that wants to focus on seeing a huge project through to its completion.

The question every PC enthusiast is asked most often is usually a variation on the theme of "why?" "Why on earth would you want to build a PC into an old Commodore 64?" "Why do you need to make your PC so much faster when it's fast enough already?" "Just how bored do you have to be to do that?" In fact, the whole notion of being a "PC enthusiast" is completely alien to anyone who isn't one. This is understandable to an extent, but there's actually no reason to think of PCs as being different from any other hobby.

For us, PCs aren't about writing up reports or online banking. In fact, for some of us they're not even about playing the latest games—although high-resolution 3D graphics can always benefit from more computing power. To us, PCs are a hobby, where you can explore new areas of technology, see what they're capable of, and have the very latest thing in your own home. When it comes down to it, it's no more unexplainable than collecting stamps, building radio-controlled cars, or any other hobby.

I put a lot of the technology aspect down to the under-privileged kid syndrome. Today's generation of PC lovers grew up with frustrating machines that, after taking 20 minutes to load a game from tape, would either crash or display an almost implausibly low-resolution game in the color palette from a child's set of wax crayons. You could, however, guarantee that there would be at least one kid at school whose dad had an

expensive proper computer that would do everything in real colors. At this point, envy kicked in.

It's the same school of thought that goes with retro toy collecting. It's often the kids that only had a couple of Transformers when they were little that are now buying Optimus Prime for $200 apiece on eBay. Having grown up with one of the worst computers in the history of mankind, I'm now making up for it by spending vast quantities of my disposable income on making sure I have the very latest computer gear.

There's also an elitist aspect to it: that smug feeling of satisfaction that goes with knowing you've built something that's superior to the average PC. Not only that, but you'll also want to compete with other enthusiast's PCs. Multi-player gaming events are huge now, and if you're taking your PC along, you want it to be something that you can show off to everyone else, whether it has distinctive looks or awesome power. Or both.

Finally, one of the other major reasons for the customization and modding phenomenon is that it's great to set yourself a project sometimes, just like sticking together a Tamiya model kit over a weekend, building a wall in the garden, or even making a film from start to finish. Designing and building your own PC from scratch taps the creative part of your brain that wants to focus on seeing a huge project through to its completion, finishing off with an awesome end result that you'll feel proud of for months to come.

Below: **Building your own PC from scratch gives you the same feeling of satisfaction as finishing a Tamiya model.**

Right: **If you ever had to put up with graphics like this as a child, you'll want to make sure it never happens again.**

Left: **It'll take months of hard work to build a PC into a truck, but it will turn heads.**

Above: **PC enthusiasm comes from the same school of thought as retro toy collecting, except that you can actually do something with the end result.**

Right: **Your PC doesn't have to just do practical things like online banking and word processing.**

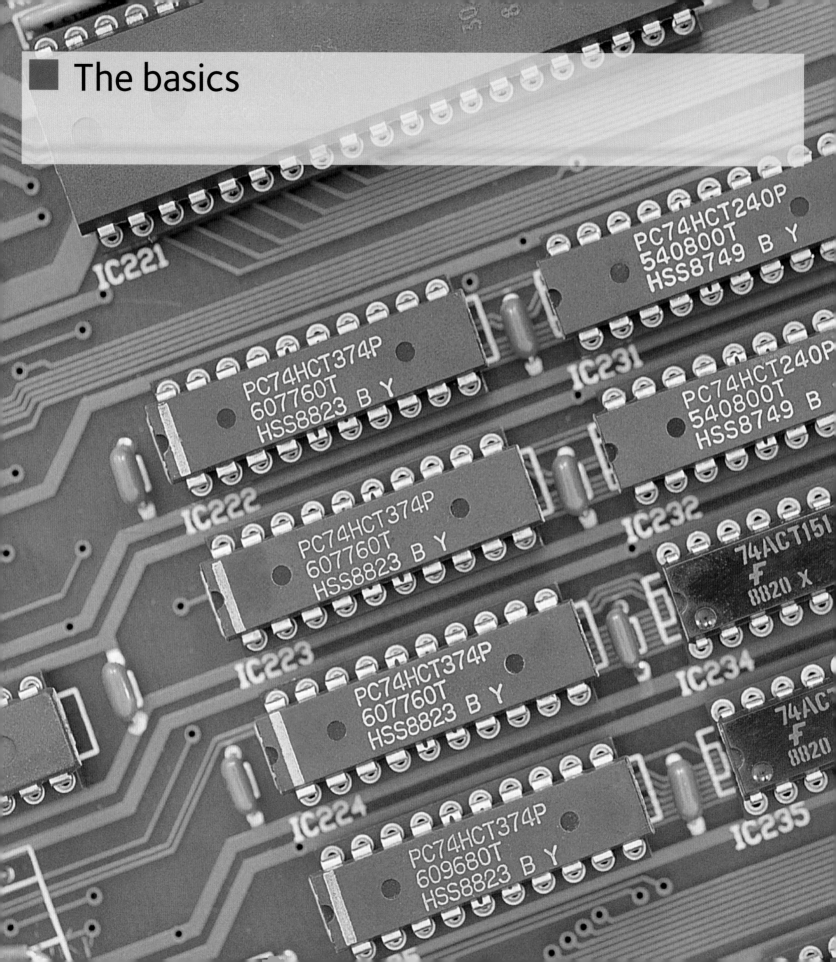

The basics

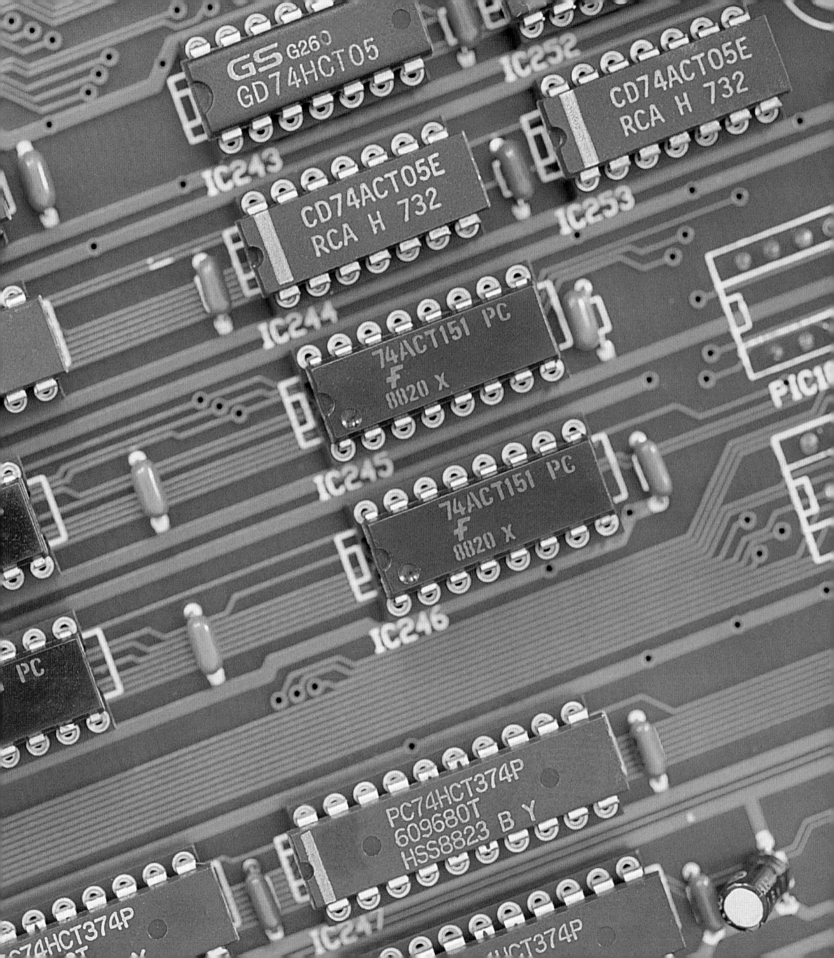

022 > 023

Processors

> The CPU can contain hundreds of millions of transistors in less than one square inch of silicon.

Your central processing unit (CPU) is arguably the most important part of your PC. In fact, it's so important that you'll find many people mistakenly calling the PC system unit the CPU. Your CPU is infinitely more complicated than a combustion engine, and it can contain hundreds of millions of transistors in less than one square inch of silicon. If you can get your head around that, then you're doing better than I am.

As you probably know, the CPU speed is generally measured in MHz or GHz (the clock speed, or the speed at which the processor can execute instructions). However, with a 2.6GHz Athlon 64 FX 55 now almost the same price as a 3.73GHz Pentium Extreme Edition, you know there must be something up. In order to explain this disparity, we need to go over the basics of how CPUs work and what makes them different.

Look at one of today's processors, and you'll see either a brown or green square with a smaller metal square on top of it. The actual processor, however, is hidden underneath the metal cover (called a heat spreader), which as the name implies, is there to help dissipate heat. If you took this piece of metal off (which you shouldn't do under any circumstances!), you'd see a much smaller chip, called the die, which is your actual processor. It might not look like much, but inside this die are millions of transistors, which make up a small set of logical parts.

All of these parts join together to do the job of processing data instructions as rapidly and efficiently as possible. As you probably already know, your computer processes data by breaking it down in to a string of binary numbers (ones or zeroes). An instruction is just a string of these numbers that has been assigned a particular purpose. At the moment there's an instruction

set (called x86), which, like an elementary table, defines what each instruction actually does. This is what Intel, AMD and all other desktop processor manufacturers follow in order to make PCs do the same things.

To process these instructions, your processor needs a set of registers. Registers are small amounts of memory, usually no more than four bytes, which store data and move it around temporarily. One of these registers is called the Program Counter (PC), and this part directs the processor toward the data in the system memory.

Once your processor has found that data, your CPU's instruction fetcher will retrieve it and pass it on to your CPU's instruction decoder. In turn, this will then work out exactly what this instruction is and will pass it on to your CPU's execution unit for processing. Once this instruction has been executed, your CPU can then start to process the next one.

And this is where things get interesting. Because your CPU can only process one instruction at a time, most of the development in processors centers around speeding up the instruction queuing process. This process is called pipelining, and it largely dictates the differences between Intel and AMD processors.

A pipeline is simply a queue of instructions awaiting execution. Effective pipelining depends on your CPU being able to reliably predict what the next instruction will be. In the old days of CPUs, pipelines were very short. The classic Pentium III processor, for example, had a ten-stage pipeline, meaning that only ten instructions could be held in the queue at one time. Having a short pipeline can be beneficial if your PC is doing lots of different things at once, as the pipeline will have to be cleared if your CPU is told to do something it hadn't predicted, slowing down the whole process.

Below: **Today's processors have a metal heat spreader on top of the actual processor.**

Right: **The older Athlon XP chips left the die exposed. That little rectangle in the middle is your whole CPU.**

Above: **CPUs look a bit like a piece of modern art inside, but believe it or not, this is the actual interior of a Pentium 4's die.**

Left: **A 2.6GHz Athlon 64 FX 55 costs almost the same amount of money as a 3.73GHz Pentium Extreme Edition, but it's not just the fancy box that you're paying for.**

Processors—Pipelines and floating point units

> It's debatable whether AMD or Intel has the best FPU in their chips, and a lot of it depends on which type of benchmark you run.

Having a deeper pipeline can be beneficial if your PC is doing repetitive tasks in which instructions can be safely predicted. A common example of this is media encoding, where the CPU is repeatedly applying the same algorithms to, say, convert an AVI video file into a WMV file.

This is the main difference between AMD's Athlon 64 and Intel's Pentium 4 (as well as the Pentium D and Extreme Edition). The Athlon 64 has a shorter 12-stage pipeline, which means that it's comparably more efficient at a lower clock speed, unless it's doing something that's both repetitive and processor-intensive. On the other hand, Intel's current processor architecture, called NetBurst, currently has a huge 31-stage pipeline in the latest chips, using Intel's branch prediction technology to try and predict the next instructions as efficiently as possible.

The upshot of this is twofold. First, Intel's chips are faster at repetitive jobs such as media encoding, while AMD's chips are generally quicker at other tasks. Second, because the Intel chips are doing comparatively less work at their clock speed, they can be clocked at a higher GHz rating. This is why the Pentium 4 chip can be found at 3.73GHz, while the Athlon 64 only goes up to 2.6GHz. This is also why the Athlon 64 chips are given a performance rating (4000+ for example)—so that people don't think it's going to be a slower chip than the Pentium 4.

A lot of cynics reckon that Intel did this purely to get higher gigahertz ratings and mislead the public into buying what were perceived as faster chips. They would probably be right. Since then, Intel has adopted a model number policy, which ranks the Intel processors according to their features rather than their clock speed.

It's also worth noting that Intel's mobile Pentium M processor is a kind of hybrid of the Pentium III and Pentium 4 technologies, combining the Pentium III's

shallower pipeline with the extra features of the Pentium 4, such as SSE2 and SSE3 (we'll come to these later). Offering the best of both worlds, while consuming less power and producing less heat, it has led many people to believe that Intel's next generation of processors will be based on the Pentium M rather than the Pentium 4. Some companies, such as AOpen, have already started producing desktop motherboards for the Pentium M.

One major advantage of the Pentium 4 architecture for enthusiasts, though, is that Pentium 4 chips are often much easier to overclock than Athlon 64 chips, for exactly the same reasons.

Another difference between the types of processor is the strength of their floating point unit (FPU). To explain, there are two types of calculation that your processor will do. The first are integer operations, which involve only whole numbers. The second are floating point operations, which involve calculations using numbers with decimal places. It's the latter that cause the most pain for processors, as they're much more complicated. This is why today's processors have at least one dedicated FPU inside, as well as the central arithmetic logic unit (ALU).

It's debatable whether AMD or Intel has the best FPU in their chips, and a lot of it depends on which type of benchmark you run. SiSoft's synthetic benchmark, Sandra, consistently shows the Intel chips to be ahead in its specific FPU tests. The FPU becomes particularly important, however, when it comes to games. 3D graphics calculations demand a lot of floating-point math and it was the pioneering 3D game, Quake, that was the first mainstream program to specifically require a processor with an FPU to run. This is also where the processors in VIA's EPIA motherboards really fall down. Even now, they still have a comparatively poor FPU, which is why you'll never see an EPIA gaming system, and also why VIA doesn't put accelerated graphics port (AGP) slots on its motherboards.

Below: **With a huge 31-stage pipeline, the latest Pentium 4 processors excel at repetitive processing tasks.**

Below Left: **With the Pentium III's shallower pipeline and all the good stuff from the Pentium 4, Intel's Pentium M laptop chip offers the perfect combination.**

Above left: **With such comparatively poor FPUs in VIA's processors, you're never going to see an EPIA gaming system.**

Above right: **With a much shorter 12-stage pipeline, the Athlon 64 can be much quicker with a slower gigahertz rating, but it's often not as overclockable.**

Right: **SiSoft's Sandra benchmarks shows the Intel CPUs to have a superior FPU.**

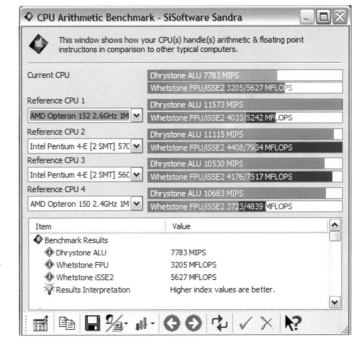

026 > 027

Processors—
Instructions and cache

> Level 2 cache has become
the most important factor
in desktop processors.
Chips with a lot of it
come at a high price.

The other parts of the CPU that can make a big difference are the amount of cache and the extra instructions, such as MMX and SSE. Let's start with the cache, which is basically a small amount of memory on the CPU to which the CPU can load data from your PC's system memory for quicker access. It's quicker firstly because it's physically closer to the CPU, but mainly because it operates much faster than your system's memory. In fact, it usually runs at about the same speed as the CPU.

There are three types of cache: Level 1, Level 2, and Level 3. The Level 1 cache is the closest to the CPU, which makes it the most efficient type for quick access. This is where your CPU will shunt any data for temporary storage so that it can be quickly pulled back in when needed. However, the amount of Level 1 cache on a processor is very small (128KB on the Athlon 64, and even less on the Pentium 4), simply because having more cache this close to the CPU can actually slow things down.

Basically, with more cache, there are more overheads from shunting data back and forth. You want to minimize these kinds of overheads as much as possible, and this is why you need a second reservoir of cache to store the data that the Level 1 cache can't accommodate. This is called the Level 2 cache in standard desktop processors, and the Level 3 cache on the Xeon and Pentium 4 Extreme Edition processors. Basically, the further away the cache from the CPU, the higher the level, and the less performance hit you'll get from having that additional cache. This is why the Xeon and Pentium 4 Extreme edition CPUs have up to 2MB of Level 3 cache, while the standard Pentium 4 has between 256KB and 1MB, depending on when it was produced.

Level 1 cache is still very important, and the lack of it is one of the main reasons why Intel's Celeron processors aren't as quick as Intel's flagship CPUs. You don't want too much of it, but you definitely want some.

However, it's the Level 2 cache that has become the most important factor in desktop processors. Chips with a lot of it, such as the Athlon 64 FX series always come with a price premium, but they usually offer much quicker performance. Often, large amounts of cache are used to compensate for other parts of the processor that might bog down. Intel, for example, increased the amount of cache on the Pentium 4 from 512KB to 1MB after it had increased the number of stages in the pipeline (otherwise known as the Prescott core). In this case, having the extra cache may not make your chip faster, as you have other overheads to consider.

Another way to make a CPU faster is to use instructions such as MMX and SSE. These are basically ways of making your processor do more. SSE, for example, stands for "streaming SIMD extensions," and SIMD stands for single-instruction, multiple data (one acronym is never enough!). All this means is that a program can send much more data in just one instruction, which the processor can then process in one go, making the whole instruction process much quicker. The MMX and SSE instructions were specifically intended to speed up multimedia and 3D graphics calculations.

The drawback to this is that you need software that can take advantage of these specific instructions, and getting this software out is always a gradual process. There's plenty of older software, for example, that can't take advantage of Intel's SSE3 technology at the time of writing, so having the very latest instructions in your CPU won't necessarily make your PC quicker. Most CPUs today come with at least SSE2 compatibility anyway, but instruction-compatibility is always something to look out for in processor development.

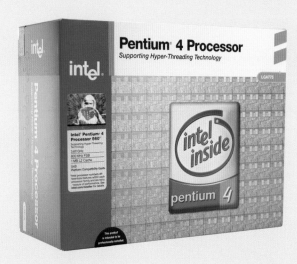

Left: **Intel's Pentium M has loads of Level 2 cache, which you can see taking up most of the CPU on the left.**

Below—top down: **The lack of Level 1 cache is one of the major factors that makes Intel's Celeron chip slower. Intel's Prescott chips have a huge 1MB of Level 2 cache, which helps to make up for their longer pipelines. High-level chips, such as Intel's Xeon processors, have buckets of Level 3 cache.**

028 > 029

Processors— multi-processing and 64-bit CPUs

> 64-bit computing is the future, but that future is still some way off.

One of the problems with current 32-bit processor technology is that it's getting harder and harder to increase raw processor speed in the face of heat and power consumption issues. As a result, the processor manufacturers are now looking to a new generation of processors, centered on 64-bit computing and multi-processing technologies. Let's start with the latter, which is old news to the server and workstation world, but a newcomer to the average desktop PC.

The idea of multi-processing is that with more than one processor, you can offload some of the work to one processor, leaving your other processor to work with everything else that much quicker. Having two processors won't actually double your performance as you might expect, but it will significantly speed up any software that's been coded to take advantage of multi-processing.

The way it works is simple. A program's processes are split up into a series of code threads, and usually your processor can only work on one thread at a time. If, however, your program has been coded to split its threads of code across two processors, then it will run much faster. The common term for this is "multi-threaded software." There isn't much of it available at the moment, but it's starting to become much more mainstream. Video-encoding programs such as TMPGEnc are already taking advantage of it.

So why does this matter to you? Simply because both Intel and AMD are trying to push the PC industry further into multi-threading. The first step was Intel's Hyper-Threading technology, which splits one Pentium 4 into two "virtual" CPUs. This works on the theory that two threads are rarely the same, and as such can use different parts of the processor. What Hyper-Threading does is tap into any unused resources in your CPU, setting them to work on other threads that can use them. This isn't as quick as having two CPUs, but if your software's coded for it, it can offer vastly improved performance.

Hyper-Threading has been around for a good few years now, but the big news at the moment is the advent of "dual core" processors, which really do give you two processors—two dies in one CPU package—bringing full-on multi-threading into the mainstream. There's still not a lot of software that will take advantage of this, and with the exception of an elusive version of *Quake III*, there aren't any games either. However, multi-processing is starting to become much more common. The next generation of games consoles will be based on multi-processor technology, PC applications are beginning to come onboard, and it's inevitable that multi-threaded software will become the norm before long.

The same is also true for 64-bit software, although this is actually even thinner on the ground. Both Intel and AMD's latest desktop processors will run in both 32-bit and 64-bit modes, but you'll need a 64-bit operating system, such as Windows XP Professional x64 Edition to make it run in 64-bit mode. AMD is claiming that even your 32-bit software will get a performance boost from running on a 64-bit operating system, but based on current tests these boosts are very small, and also few and far between.

64-bit software is already starting to appear though. There's already a 64-bit patch for the game *Far Cry*, which adds some graphical enhancements (none of which look like they couldn't have been done with a 32-bit processor), and more look set to follow. At the moment, though, it's all a bit of a gimmick. You'll find that a 32-bit processor with the standard version of Windows XP will do everything you need. 64-bit computing is the future, but that future is still some way off.

Basically, if you're buying a new processor then you may as well buy a 64-bit model, but if you've already got a high-spec 32-bit processor, then there's no real need to upgrade it just yet.

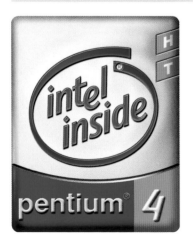

Above: **The initials "HT" on the Pentium 4 logo stand for "Hyper-Threading," which means that it will create a second virtual CPU.**

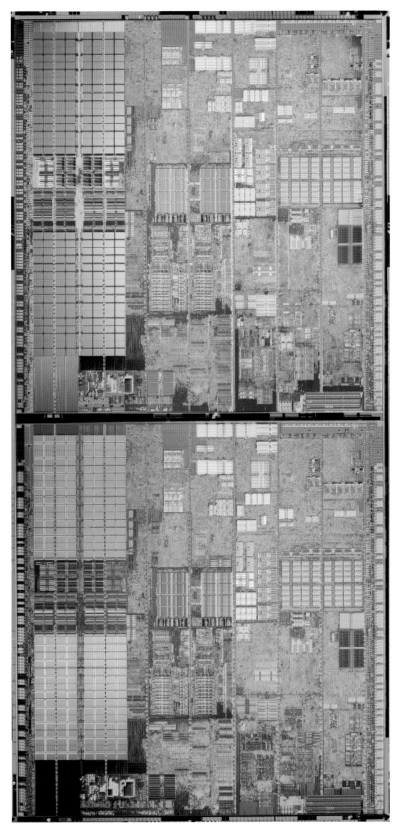

Left: Looking inside Intel's new dual-core Pentium Extreme Edition you can see that it genuinely contains two complete processors.

Right: There's already a 64-bit patch for the game *Far Cry*, but the differences hardly kick it out of the 32-bit league.

Below: With two cores, AMD's new Athlon 64 X2 chip will be quicker when more multi-threaded software turns up.

030 > 031

Motherboards— buses and sockets

> The front side bus and the multiplier form the most important basis for overclocking.

Ignored by many in favor of more exciting parts like the processor or graphics card, the motherboard should actually be your first consideration. It dictates not only what brand of processor you use, but also the exact type of processor and how fast it will be, as well as the type of memory and graphics card you need. Your motherboard establishes the kind of PC you can build now, and the kind you can upgrade to in the future.

There are lots of things to consider here, but let's start with your choice of processor. Firstly, check what type of socket it uses—you need to make your PC as future-proof as possible, so choose one with the latest socket and you may be able to upgrade your processor somewhere along the line before your motherboard is obsolete. At the moment, the current desktop sockets are Socket 939 for AMD Athlon 64 and Athlon FX chips, LGA775 for Intel's desktop chips, and Socket 479 for its mobile CPUs. The ones to avoid are Socket 478, Socket 754 and Socket 940. While they'll still run current chips, you won't be able to get an upgrade out of them later.

The next thing to look for is the front side bus speed, which will also dictate your choice of processor. The front side bus basically carries data from your CPU to the other parts of your computer, such as your memory and peripheral component interconnect (PCI) cards, and by increasing its speed, you not only increase the speed of your CPU but also the speed of the interface between the CPU and the rest of your PC. Your CPU is then given a specific figure to multiply the front side bus by to get its final speed. So with a 200MHz front side bus, you would need a 12x multiplier for a 2.4GHz processor. The front side bus and the multiplier form the most important basis of overclocking, which we'll come to later. It's also worth noting, however, that Intel's latest chips have what's known as a "quad pumped" front side bus, which puts through four times as much data per clock cycle to increase performance.

This is why the specifications on the boxes will proudly display figures such as "1,066MHz front side bus," when the actual figure you'll be working with is 266MHz.

AMD's chips don't have a front side bus, as they have a memory controller actually built into the CPU. However, they still have an interface with the motherboard, called the HyperTransport bus, which lets any HyperTransport-enabled parts talk directly to each other. It's a superior technology to the front side bus, but it works in pretty much the same way. Basically, it's always good to get a motherboard that supports the fastest front side bus or HyperTransport technology, as these will still support the older chips and still give you some headroom to upgrade in the future.

All of this will be controlled by the main chip on your motherboard, which is commonly called the "Northbridge." Motherboards will all be based on a chipset, and this will comprise a Northbridge chip for controlling the speed and bandwidth of your components, and a Southbridge chip for controlling peripheral add-ons, such as your USB 2 and FireWire ports, and for running any onboard sound. It's the Northbridge that the chipset is always named after, mainly because you often find the same Southbridge on different chipsets. This is also worth looking out for before you buy a motherboard, as there are pros and cons to some of the different brands and models.

Intel's latest chipsets, for example, support 7.1-surround sound in the Southbridge and a 1,066Hz front side bus in the Northbridge, but they also only have one integrated drive electronics (IDE) channel, which can be a problem if you want to upgrade your motherboard, but not your hard drive and CD drive too. NVIDIA's latest nForce chips are well worth a look. Not only do they support all the latest front side bus speeds, but some also feature the company's SLI technology, which lets you run two graphics cards in parallel (we'll go into why on page 48).

Short on 3D speed? A motherboard based on NVIDIA's nForce4 SLI chipset will let you run two expensive graphics cards at once.

Above & right: **Intel's LGA775 socket is currently the most up-to-date Intel socket around.**

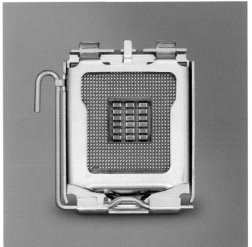

Left above: **A Northbridge chip, which controls communications between the major components (CPU, RAM, hard disk, graphics card) slotted into the motherboard.**
Left: **The Southbridge chip handles audio, USB 2 and FireWire ports, and any other communications with external devices.**
Right: **AMD's Athlon 64 chips have an integrated memory controller.**

DDR Memory Controller

L1 Instruction Cache

"Hammer" Processor Core

L1 Data Cache

L2 Cache

HyperTransport™

032 > 033

Motherboards—slots

> Think about the components you want to add, where you want to put them, and check if there's anything that might prevent this.

NVIDIA wasn't the first graphics company to decide that two cards could offer more performance than one, and it certainly won't be the last. ATI now has its own dual graphics setup called CrossFire. However, this differs from SLI in the slots it requires.

Both SLI and Crossfire use the latest addition to the motherboard slot family: PCI-Express (PCI-E). PCI-E is a replacement for the age-old AGP and PCI slots that you used to find on most motherboards. Since 1997, the AGP slot has been the standard slot for graphics cards, taking over from the PCI slots which are still used for peripheral add-ons such as modems and sound cards. AGP remains a fast technology—and it's certainly not dead yet—but PCI-E offers several advantages, the principal ones being higher bandwidth and the potential to scale that bandwidth upwards.

Basically, your motherboard chipset will offer a specific number of "lanes" for each of your PCI-E slots, each of which can cope with 500MB of data every second. The more lanes your slot has, the more data the card plugged into it can send to the motherboard at once. Standard setups usually have around 20 lanes, 16 for the main graphics slot, and another four for single-lane PCI-E slots (the little ones).

However, the dual-graphics boards split this differently. It's fair to say that graphics technology hasn't got to a point where you need 16 lanes yet (you won't see any jump from eight, as the graphics cards simply aren't fast enough to use the interface). As a result, NVIDIA's nForce4 SLI chipset provides two full-size PCI-E slots that use eight lanes each. ATI's CrossFire does the same with the two slots, while Intel's E7525 Xeon chipset provides two full-size slots, one with eight lanes and one with just four (although even four lanes are enough to run SLI sufficiently). SLI will work with any of these configurations, as long as NVIDIA offers to provide driver support for the chipset. CrossFire, however, specifically requires two eight-lane slots.

At the moment, PCI-E is still in its infancy, and you're really not going to see a difference by upgrading to a PCI-E system now. Arguably, if you're buying a new motherboard to replace your old one, then your best bet is to look at a board that offers the best of both worlds, with both new and old slots and sockets to soften the blow of upgrading.

There are plenty of boards that offer older processor sockets with PCI-E slots, so that you don't necessarily need a new processor, and there are also

Left: **NVIDIA's nForce Pro** motherboard ships with the company's nTune software for overclocking.

Above: **VIA's PT880 Pro** supports the right mix of today's and yesterday's technologies, making it perfect for upgraders.

boards with new processor sockets and older memory sockets (the latest Intel boards only support DDR 2 memory, see page 34). Examples of this include the Gigabyte GA-8I865PEM-775, which offers an LGA775 CPU with Intel's older 865 chipset, and supports regular DDR memory. Boards based on VIA's PT880 Pro chipset, such as Gigabyte's GA-8VT880P Combo are also worth a look, as this chipset is compatible with AGP and PCI-E slots, as well as both DDR and DDR 2 memory. It can even have all of them on the same board.

Layout and cooling

The next thing to look at is the cooling technology used on the motherboard, especially if you want to either overclock your PC or even build a silent system. An example of the latter is Abit's new Silent OTES heatpipe system, allowing the removal of all fans from the board.

At the other end of the scale, Abit has its Fatal1ty motherboards, which come with five fans for super-cool overclocking. Many motherboards are particularly geared toward overclocking, and even come with hardcore heatsinks and utilities to help you along. There are also particular features that will help with overclocking, such

as an AGP/PCI lock, or the capability to drop your CPU's multiplier and alter your memory timings.

Finally, the last thing to look at is the board's layout. Even today, some boards look like they've been designed by an orangutan with a soldering iron, so think about the components you want to add, where you want to put them, and check if there's anything that might prevent this. Sore points might include the close proximity of large capacitors to the CPU socket, which could prevent you mounting a large heatsink. You also want to distribute the heat as evenly as possible, so make sure that there's plenty of room between your graphics card, your CPU, and your memory for that matter.

As with all of these things, it's best to check out plenty of reviews in magazines and on websites before you buy, as these will be able to tell you which boards have a greater overclocking ceiling, as well as providing the most detailed and up-to-date information on all the other features of specific motherboards.

Above: **Look for silent coolers such as Abit's Silent OTES if you want to build a quieter system, although this cooler also relies on airflow from the CPU cooler, so don't mix it with a water cooling system.**

Right: **With five cooling fans, Abit's Fatal1ty range of motherboards is great for overclockers.**

Right: **ATI's CrossFire technology requires two eight-lane PCI-E slots.**

Memory

> Expensive, high-end memory is only of use to overclockers who can push up their front side bus to a speed that can take advantage of it.

Looking more like handbag accessories than bits of circuit boards, today's memory modules are sleek, shiny, and more often than not, extremely expensive. However, just because a module is more expensive doesn't necessarily mean it's going to be any quicker, and there are many factors to consider before spending large amounts of cash on a matched pair of OCZ 1GHz DIMMs.

The first, and most obvious, thing to consider is what type of memory you need for your system. As a general rule, Athlon 64 motherboards support 184-pin DDR memory modules, while the latest Pentium 4 motherboards (but not the earlier ones) support 240-pin DDR 2 modules. DDR and DDR 2 modules not only differ physically (you can't put a DDR module in a DDR 2 slot), but they're also quite different technology-wise. DDR stands for double data rate, which means that it transfers data at both the beginning and the end of each clock, effectively giving you double the data rate per MHz. DDR 2 memory, meanwhile, doesn't actually transfer four times as much data per MHz, but is basically a souped up type of DDR memory that requires less power and runs at a lower voltage. This allows it to be clocked much higher than standard DDR memory.

The next thing to consider is the memory's bandwidth, which is measured in several different ways. The most usual one is data throughput, measured in megabytes per second. PC2100 memory, for example, can handle 2,100MB per second. However, this is sometimes also measured in MHz, which is a hangover from how memory bandwidth used to be measured. PC133 memory, for example, ran at 133MHz. It's also worth bearing in mind that the MHz rating of DDR (and DDR 2) memory often refers to the effective bandwidth that you'd get from doubling it—so while PC2100 memory actually runs at 133MHz, it's sometimes sold as 266MHz.

You can also double the potential data throughput of your memory by using a dual-channel motherboard (most of today's motherboards offer this). By using two identical DIMMs in the right slots, your motherboard will then access these in parallel/serial to double the bandwidth. This does, however, require both modules to have the same amount of memory, and preferably the same specifications too, which is why many companies sell matched sets of dual channel modules.

It's very easy to get caught in the trap of believing that more bandwidth will make your PC faster, but remember that you can only go as fast as your slowest component. The speed of your memory will ultimately be determined by your system's front side bus, so if your processor only runs on an 533MHz front side bus, then you're not going to see any performance increase from having dual channel PC3200 (effectively 800MHz) memory.

When it comes down to it, expensive, high-bandwidth memory is only of use to overclockers who can push up their front side bus to a speed that can take advantage of it. On the other hand, you can run this memory at any speed below its maximum rating if you want to, and it's worth considering as a future-proof investment, so that you don't have to upgrade your memory and your processor next time around.

The next thing to look at on your memory is its latency. This is usually quoted in terms of four digits, such as 8-3-2-2.5, which are usually in order of tRAS-tRCD-tRP-CAS. All of these unpronounceable acronyms refer to the memory's latency timings. We won't go into these in detail at this stage, but the most important and commonly quoted spec is the CAS (sometimes referred to as CL) rating. The lower this is, the faster your memory will be. This is basically the number of clock cycles it will take for an instruction to go from the memory controller and through the memory. On DDR memory, you want this to be CL2.5 or lower. DDR 2 memory, meanwhile, still has a comparatively high latency compared to DDR modules, so CL4 DDR 2 memory is fine.

Finally, the last thing you should note is that those bits of metal on your memory make pretty much no difference at all. They don't offer nearly enough material for effective heat dissipation, and their main job is to make the memory look "exclusive." Similarly, having memory with flashing LEDs won't make your PC any faster. They just look particularly cool, especially Corsair's programmable XMS XPERT range.

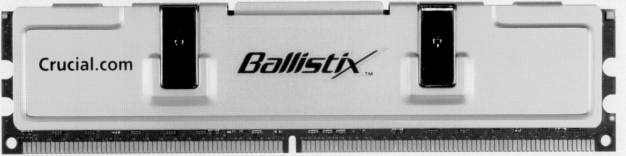

Far left: **Corsair's light-up XMS XPERT memory is** gimmicky, but lots of fun. Left: **Corsair XMS2.** Below left: **Gold heat spreaders look fantastic,** but they don't actually do very much. Below: **Kingston HyperX and Geil Ultra Platinum PC4400.** Most memory companies sell matched sets of dual channel modules.

036 > 037

Hard drives

> You will see many websites talk about modding your hard drive. Don't ever try to do this unless you really know what you're doing.

It's difficult to get excited about hard drives in the same way that you can about processors and graphics cards. There's just no getting around the fact that they're plain silver bricks, put to shame by other more glamorous computer components. However, much like every superhero's alter ego, there's something incredibly useful underneath that dull exterior.

Depending on what you do with your PC, the hard drive is the part that could make all the difference. A fast hard drive could cut up to 20 seconds off the loading time between levels in the latest games, make Windows load up in half the time, and may do wonders for photo and video editing software, too.

There are plenty of rumors to ignore about hard drives. The first is that the speed of the interface will actually make them faster. Modern motherboards support a transfer rate of 3Gb/second from a SATA 2 hard drive, which looks fantastic compared to the 133Mb/second you get from an IDE hard drive, but in reality your hard drive is never going to reach anywhere near that kind of speed, so that rating is entirely nominal. It's also worth looking for extra cache (around 8MB will be fine), as well as command queuing technology, which can speed things up a bit.

The actual speed of your hard drive will be determined by its rotational spin speed, which is measured in rpm. Most hard drives today come with a 7,200rpm spin speed, but it's still worth checking the specs out, as you don't want to end up with a sluggish 5,400rpm drive. The exception to this rule is laptop hard drives, which haven't quite caught up with desktop hard drives yet.

Of course, you can go beyond 7,200rpm. Western Digital's Raptor hard drive boasts a phenomenal spin speed of 10,000rpm. It's intended for use in servers, but with its SATA interface it can also be used in desktop PCs. These are considered to be the ultimate enthusiast's hard drive, although in reality the performance gains are still minimal, and they only come in sizes of 36GB and 74GB at the time of writing. They are the fastest drives out there, but

whether they're worth quadruple the standard price is debatable to all but the incredibly affluent.

Raptors are noisy too, and if noise is a priority then it's worth checking out a quieter alternative such as Samsung's SpinPoint P80 drives, which are barely audible in use. It's also worth noting that not all 7,200rpm drives are as fast as each other (the Samsung is notably slower), so it's worth checking out several reviews of the latest hard drive models before making a purchase.

In the enthusiast's market you'll also see systems marketed with hard drives in RAID configuration. RAID stands for "redundant array of inexpensive disks," and it's a way of linking hard drives together to act as an identical backup of a drive (RAID 1) or to act as one big unit of hard drive space (called RAID 0). The latter is also referred to as "striping" and is supposed to make your hard drives even faster, although again the speed difference is hardly noticeable, if it's even there. RAID is really a technology for keeping solid backups in servers and workstations, and it's debatable whether it's really needed on the PC. Saying this is often considered heresy in the enthusiast community, though, and you'll find many people who disagree with me.

In terms of size, most people now consider 80GB the bare minimum, and once you start filling your system with audio files, games, digital photos, video files, and applications, even that is going to seem too small very quickly. 160GB is a more sensible capacity, and you should consider going higher if you plan to do a lot of audio or video work with your PC.

One last word of warning. You will see many websites that talk about modding your hard drive, perhaps by adding a window in the top or sticking some LEDs in it. You can understand why; hard drive aesthetics are far from appealing. However, don't ever try to do this unless you really know what you're doing. Even then, I'd seriously advise you to forget it—hard drives are very sensitive and delicate, and they tend to stop working if you tamper with them.

Far left: **They might be a fundamental part of your system, but there's no doubt that hard drives rival power supplies for being your PC's dullest-looking component.**
Left: **The aptly named Raptor is the fastest drive on the block, and the ridges down its sides make it stand out, too.**

Above: **Hard drives look much more interesting inside, but don't even think about fitting in a window. Ever.**
Right: **RAID controllers let you link hard drives together to either increase performance or create a backup.**

038 > 039

Power supplies

> You can't just add up your rails' power output to get the total wattage, as your PSU won't be able to output that power when it's supplying all the rails at once.

The humble power supply unit (PSU) is often the most overlooked part of a PC, with many people making do with the one that came with their case, or the cheap 400W one they saw on sale. You probably think you don't need a decent power supply. After all, you wouldn't pay out loads of extra cash for a better-quality power pack for your games console, so why should your PC be any different? The answer is that PCs are split into several components, all of which make varying, sometimes immense, demands of your power supply. If these don't get enough power then your system can become unstable, and end up crashing and restarting itself.

In more detail, your power supply has several different rails, each of which supplies a different voltage to the various parts of your PC. There are quite a few rails, but the most important ones are the +12V, +5V, and +3.3V, and your power supply will be able to supply a certain amount of current (amps) to each rail. A decent PSU will have these ratings somewhere in the specifications, and from this you can work out that rail's maximum wattage by multiplying the current by the rail's voltage. In simple terms: Voltage multiplied by amps equals wattage, so if your 12V rail is rated at 19A, then it has an output of 228W.

Once you know the wattage of your rails, you can then work out what components will be satisfied by that power supply. For example, NVIDIA recommends a 400W PSU with a 12V rail rated at a minimum of 26A for its GeForce 7800 GTX card, so this is what you need to look for in your power supply specifications to run this card.

One other thing to bear in mind is that the total wattage quoted for a power supply is often a nominal figure based on an unrealistic PC specification. What's more, you can't just add up the sum total of your rails' power output in watts to get the total wattage, as your PSU won't be able to output that amount of power when it's supplying all the rails at once. This is why some power supplies also come with a "combined power output" rating, which is usually a combination of both the 3.3V and 5V rails. This is a more realistic figure for your PSU's total wattage.

Unfortunately there aren't any hard and fast rules to which rail a component takes, and the information isn't always easily available. However, the most important ones to know are those for the CPU and graphics card. Newer processors (from the Pentium 4 and Athlon 64 onwards) use the 12V rail, which is why you get the extra four-pin 12V connector on newer motherboards, as well as the standard ATX block connector. Meanwhile, an AGP graphics card will take most of its power from the 3.3V rail, although if it has any Molex connectors for extra power, then these will drain extra power from the 5V and 12V rails too. These are also where your hard drives and optical drives will take their power supply.

Finally, a PCI-E graphics card that requires the extra PCI-E power connectors will also drain a lot of power from the 12V rail. Considering that this is the rail powering your CPU, you're more than likely to need two PSUs if you want to set up a dual-graphics card system.

With a bit of research on the net, you should be able to find out which rails your components will stress and then buy an appropriate power supply. It's also worth noting that these ratings always denote peak power, and that it will usually be using less than this. All the same, it's best to make sure you have enough power to accommodate everything running at full capacity, just to avoid the PC equivalent of the old *Star Trek* "the engines, she cannae take nae more" speech.

The other thing to look out for in a power supply is Power Factor Correction (PFC), which is the circuitry that shares out the power between the different rails. Your PSU should at least have passive PFC, although active PFC will do an even better job. Your components draw different amounts of power on different rails while they're working, so you want to be sure that they're getting the power when they need it.

Basically, if you're building a high-spec PC then do your research and make sure you get a power supply that's up to the job. However, this also all depends on what you want to do with your PC. The technical elite of the PC world will sneer at cheap power supplies, but the truth is that, as long as they came out in the last three or four years, they will all do the job for a simple, low-spec PC. Also, make sure you look for a PSU that conforms to the ATX12V 2.0 specification, as this will offer two 12V rails—ideal for power-hungry high-end PCI-E graphics cards.

Below: **Today's CPUs draw their power from the 12V rail, which is why newer motherboards have a 12V power connector in addition to the usual ATX power connector.**

Right: **An AOpen power supply unit.**

Below right: **The cheap PSU on eBay might look tempting, but you know absolutely nothing about its specifications and it's likely to choke at even the thought of a high-spec system.**

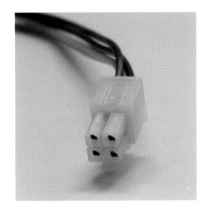

Below: **Two GeForce 6800 Ultras are going to need an incredibly powerful 12V rail. In fact, they might even need two PSUs.**

040 > 041

Graphically speaking

> The Voodoo FX chipset was based on 4MB of memory, and was able to go up to a resolution of 640 x 480 in 16-bit color.

There's no doubt that if you borrowed Doc Brown's DeLorean, traveled back to 1985, and interrupted an 8-year-old Spectrum owner's *3D Monster Maze* session to show them *Doom 3*, they'd probably end up losing their eyeballs in amazement. Computer graphics are phenomenally close to a comic book reality now, and it's all thanks to the relentless progress of the graphics card.

But graphics cards weren't always this revered. Back in 1996, the system requirements stickers on game boxes were pretty straightforward. If they said a game needed a Pentium 100 with 16MB of RAM and you had a 486 DX2/66, you could safely say that it wouldn't be playable. At this point the graphics card was very rarely even mentioned as its only job was to display things on the screen. All this changed with the advent of the 3D accelerator.

Who came up with the original idea for this is disputable. Companies in the 3D workstation arena, such as Permedia, had chipsets out before 1995, the first NVIDIA graphics chip (the NV1) appeared in 1996, and low-performance chipsets such as the S3 ViRGE and ATI Rage3D were making their way into systems by early 1997. The problem was that these either weren't compatible with most games, or they actually slowed them down! As a result, there wasn't a really successful 3D accelerator until late 1996, when the 3Dfx Voodoo FX chipset made its debut.

Based on just 4MB of memory, and only able to go up to a maximum resolution of 640 x 480 in 16-bit color, the Voodoo looks pretty feeble by today's

standards, but it was this card that made the first (and, to be honest, only) massive jump in PC graphics. Before that, 3D games had always been rendered in software by the processor, which made them look chunky, pixelated, and slightly worse than the graphics coming from Sony's first-generation PlayStation. Plugging in a Voodoo card, however, smoothed out all those pixels in *Quake*, gave you shiny floors in *Unreal*, sped up *Tomb Raider*, and made everything look simply amazing. The PC was, for the first time in history, the ultimate gaming machine.

Unlike today's graphics cards, though, the Voodoo was just a 3D card, and you needed another separate 2D card to go with it—linking them round the back with a pass-through cable. VideoLogic's PowerVR card, which finally launched a year or so later, operated along similar lines. It didn't need a pass through cable, but it plugged into a PCI slot alongside your existing card. Further competitors, such as ATI's Rage 2 and the Matrox Mystique series soon followed, but couldn't compete with the Voodoo's speed or its minimal Pentium 90/8Mb RAM system requirements.

3dfx followed it up in 1998 with the superb Voodoo2, which could go up to 800 x 600, and even reach 1,024 x 768 if you added another one with an SLI (scan line interleave) cable. It looked like 3dfx was unstoppable at this point, and in 1999 the company took things another step further with the Voodoo3, which could run 3D games at up to 1,600 x 1,200, came with a TV-out, and was also a 2D and 3D card in one. Sadly for them, trouble was coming round the corner, in the shape of NVIDIA.

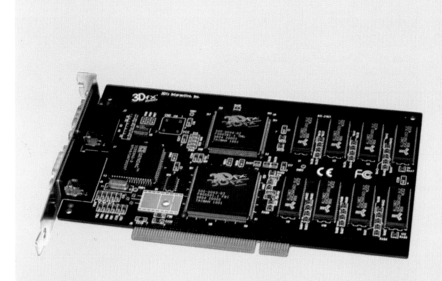

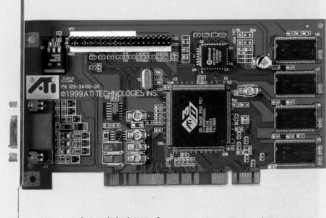

Left: **It only had 4MB of memory and a maximum resolution of 640 x 480, but the Voodoo was hot stuff back in 1997.**

Above: **ATI were big in the 2D business desktop market, but their 3D Rage series was no match for the mighty Voodoo.**

Right: **The Voodoo provided the first major leap in 3D graphics—look at the difference between** *Quake* **rendered on software (left) and hardware (right).**
Below: **Shiny floors in** *Unreal* **were only possible with a 3dfx Voodoo card.**

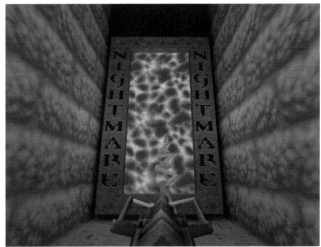

042 > 043

What has NVIDIA ever done for us?

> In 1999, NVIDIA's GeForce 256 arrived. This handled T&L, and therefore all the heavy lifting of the 3D graphics pipeline.

3dfx's reign was short lived, mainly as a result of the emergence of NVIDIA, its most aggressive competitor, which bought the company out in January 2001. Put simply, NVIDIA took 3dfx's idea and made it infinitely superior before 3dfx could work out what had hit them.

So what did NVIDIA do differently? To understand that requires a basic knowledge of how 3D graphics work. Basically, a 3D object needs to go through several processes before it appears in all its beautifully textured glory on your screen. When collected together, we call this process the graphics pipeline. This would take a whole book to describe in detail—and there are several different takes on it that shift elements from one stage to another—but in essence it works as follows.

First, the 3D scene is set up with the position of any objects, their movement, and the position and the movement of the camera, turning the basic information into a series of vertices: points in 3D space that define the objects within that space. Then comes transform and lighting (T&L)—the calculations that tell you where a 3D object (or its vertices) will be in relation to everything else, how it's changed in the view (growing larger or smaller, or changing shape), and how it will react to any lights in the scene. Next comes rasterization—filling in the vertices with real textures. Finally, we have pixel

operations, a term which encompasses a number of calculations that determine how the final object will look and behave.

The 3dfx cards only accelerated the very final stages: rasterizations and pixel operations. What they didn't do was calculate the transform and lighting (T&L). This still had to be done by the CPU. However, in 1999, NVIDIA's GeForce 256 arrived. This handled transform and lighting, and therefore all the heavy lifting of the 3D graphics pipeline, in hardware. NVIDIA was so pleased with this that it coined the term graphics processing unit (GPU) to describe it. T&L was integrated into Microsoft's DirectX 7, and ATI later followed it up in 2000 with a similar T&L-equipped graphics chip, the ATI Radeon.

These were a big hit back in the day, but you're now probably wondering why, if it was so great, you can't use a GeForce 256 card to run today's games. The reason is that having the graphics pipeline in the hardware meant that programmers were restricted to only doing what the graphics card was capable of doing. Software rendering was actually a lot more flexible, even if it turned your CPU into a stuttering wreck.

This lack of flexibility is commonly known as "fixed function" by games developers, and in an industry

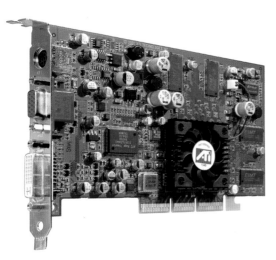

Above: **NVIDIA was so proud of the GeForce 256, that it called it a GPU, and the term has been misused to describe any graphics chip ever since.**
Left: **ATI followed up the GeForce3 with the superior Radeon 8500 with DirectX 8.1 support.**

where cool and distinctive effects can help sell games, programmers wanted more room for innovation. The response was to introduce programmable shaders into the equation, which appeared with DirectX 8 and NVIDIA's GeForce 3. Put simply, a shader is a small program that's run on the GPU to make certain operations much quicker. At the moment there are two types—pixel and vertex shaders. DirectX 8 brought us the version 1.1 models.

These provided the ability to produce some amazing effects. If you want an example, take a look at the Nature test in 3DMark2001. Even now, it has dazzling water effects and brilliant swaying grass. Later on, ATI unleashed the superior Radeon 8500, which was not only faster, but also added compatibility with DirectX 8.1. This provided the enhanced Pixel Shader 1.4.

However, this was only a taster for what was to follow. The main problem with DirectX 8's pixel and vertex shaders was that their calculations were limited to restrictive integer mathematics (i.e. no floating decimal points), and the shaders were also very short, meaning that there wasn't enough space to program them to do exactly what you wanted them to do.

More flexibility was required, and that was to come with DirectX 9.

Left: **Even now, the water effects in 3DMark2001 are dazzling, and the Special Edition added a further DirectX 8.1 pixel shader test.**
Right: ***Doom 3* in DirectX 7 and DirectX 9—guess which one's which. That's the difference that shaders make!**

More shaders and pipelines

> The most important factor in choosing a powerful graphics card is the number of pixel pipelines.

This is where everything gets confusing, because DirectX 9 has had several stages, and not all of them have been supported by both NVIDIA and ATI. At the start, the main point of DirectX 9 was to continue the good work of DirectX 8, but add floating point precision and longer shaders. With Shader Model 2, programming could be more complex, while allowing the shader more flexibility.

However, when NVIDIA released its GeForce 6-series of cards in 2004, it took this to a new level with support for DirectX 9c. This adds support for Shader Model 3, which enables a card to texture with the vertex shader. This in turn allows some incredible graphical illusions to be achieved. One example is displacement mapping, which lets you produce a realistically detailed brick wall with just a couple of polygons—the shader would then do all the texturing work, making detailed 3D graphics much faster to process, there being significantly fewer polygons to work with.

Another major part of Shader Model 3 is high dynamic range (HDR), which allows a far greater range of lighting, from blinding sunlight to dark shadowy corners. HDR isn't exclusive to Shader Model 3, and ATI cards are capable of doing it too, but DirectX 9c offers an easy route into it for programmers, which means that any game currently accessing HDR through DirectX 9c won't be able to run HDR on an ATI card. Unfortunately, at the time of writing, this applies to every HDR-compatible game out there. However, there's no doubt that ATI will have to catch up with Shader Model 3, and its next generation of chips is more than likely to support it.

The effects of HDR are incredible to behold, and you can enable it in *Far Cry* with the latest patch on a GeForce 6-series card. The lighting effects are simply stunning, and make the game beautiful to look at. On the downside, HDR also kills your frame rate unless you have a seriously powerful graphics setup to cope with it.

So what makes a powerful 3D graphics card? To start with, you've got the fundamental basics of what clock speed the GPU is running at, as well as what speed the memory is running at. GDDR3 memory, for example, is much quicker, and usually much more overclockable, too. The most important factor, however, is the number of pixel pipelines.

You can think of these as a bit like parallel processing with several CPUs. Basically, GPUs have very deep pipelines, as their functions are very predictable and they know what they're going to be doing. As a result, GPUs are much happier with parallel processing than CPUs, and there is practically no performance hit. When your graphics card is processing a pixel shader, it will break down the work into 2 x 2-pixel squares, which are called "quads," and the number of pipelines determines how many of these quads it can process at the same time. However, the number of pixel pipelines relates to the total number of pixels processed simultaneously, rather than the number of quads. So a card with eight pixel pipelines can process two quads at a time, and eight pixels. In a nutshell, the greater the number of pipelines, the quicker your graphics card will be at shader-intensive work. Your card will also have some dedicated vertex engines for vertex shaders, though these will be fewer in number. This makes sense, as there are fewer vertices in the average 3D scene than pixels.

However, bear in mind that—for the moment, at least—you get diminishing returns on the number of pipelines after a certain point. You'll notice very little performance difference between a 24-pipe GeForce 7800 GTX and a 16-pipe GeForce 6800 Ultra in most games; it's only in the really shader-intensive stuff, such as HDR at high resolutions, that cards with more pipelines really start to pull away.

Left: **NVIDIA's GeForce 6-series cards added support for Shader Model 3 and HDR.** Opposite page, above: **This preview shot of characters from *Unreal 3* shows what it will be possible to do with shaders in the near future.**

Right below: ***Far Cry* before and after HDR was enabled. The light flare can be incredibly bright.** Far right below: **DirectX 9 made the next Nature test in 3DMark03 even more impressive.**

046 > 047

Anti-aliasing and anisotropic filtering

> The greater the level of anti-aliasing, the greater the impact on performance, but it makes such an amazing difference that it's always worth enabling.

If there's one thing the PC industry loves to do, it's create overly complicated terms for things that are actually very simple. Two prime examples are anti-aliasing and anisotropic filtering, which are often talked about when it comes to graphics cards.

Let's start with anti-aliasing. This isn't anything to do with deterring people in disguise from turning up in your vicinity. It is, in fact, a fantastic tool for smoothing out the jagged edges created when you render 3D graphics. In very basic terms, it means that a diagonal line will look like a smooth diagonal line, rather than a series of steps. Anti-aliasing was one of the last things that 3dfx gave us before it sank into oblivion, and there are several different ways of doing it.

The most basic form of anti-aliasing is super-sampling. Traditionally, super-sampling works by creating a large version of the original (one of 1,600 x 1,200 pixels for a final product of 800 x 600) and then scaling it down, making the edges within the smaller image that much smoother. However, this has a massive effect on performance, so it's now been ousted for the most part in favor of another technique called multi-sampling. This works by sampling the color of the pixels on the edges of objects, and then determining the color of the surrounding pixels accordingly. Of course, the greater number of pixels you sample, the more accurate the blending will be, and you can select this in your graphics driver's display properties (2x, 4x, etc).

Admittedly, the greater the number of samples, the greater the impact on performance, but anti-aliasing makes such an amazing difference that it's always worth enabling. It not only makes games look better, but it can also make objects in the distance look more realistic. Most graphics cards also let you add a form of super-sampling on top of the usual multi-sampling anti-aliasing for the ultimate in smooth graphics quality, but this will bring all but the most ludicrously powerful mission-control PCs to their knees.

Another anti-aliasing method is temporal anti-aliasing, which alternates a different anti-aliasing pattern between frames, creating even more anti-aliasing samples. This relies on a consistently fast frame rate to fool the human eye into not seeing the flicker between frames. The minimum frame rate considered necessary for this to work is 60fps. Temporal anti-aliasing has yet to hit the mainstream, but ATI has promised support for its X800-series cards in a future driver release, and it could become an important part of anti-aliasing in the future.

Anisotropic filtering, meanwhile, is a similar smoothing feature, though it works on different elements and in different ways. The best way to think of anisotropic filtering is to think of a large, flat image that is rotating about its horizontal axis. As it rotates, the perspective changes, and with normal 3D computer calculations, this will cause the distant edges and lines to look jagged. With anisotropic filtering, however, it retains more of its proportional characteristics and looks more natural. Again, you can vary the amount of anisotropic filtering in your display properties. Sadly, it's also true that the more anisotropic filtering you have, the more it will affect your performance.

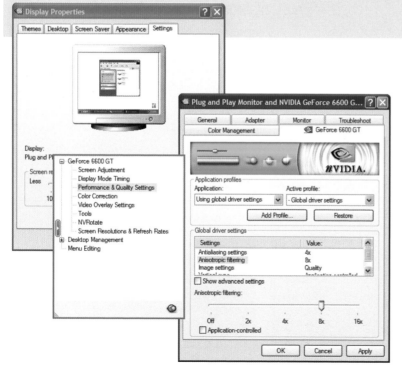

Left: You can change the amount of anti-aliasing and anisotropic filtering in your advanced display properties. Higher values look better, but expect an adverse effect on performance.

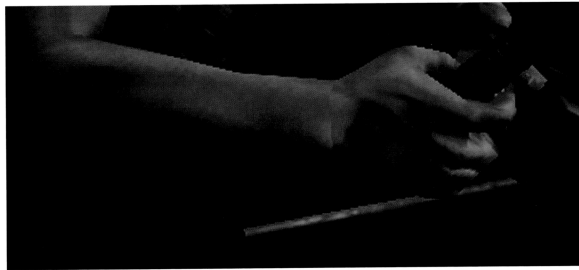

Left: **Anti-aliasing (top) smooths out jagged edges, and makes them look much more natural.**

Left: **Without anisotropic filtering, a 3D image distorts when you change its angle** Below left: **With anisotropic filtering, it retains its geometric proportions and looks more natural.**

Two heads are better than one

> To run these dual-card systems, you'll need a compatible motherboard, and that doesn't just mean any board with two full-size PCI-E slots.

As we mentioned earlier, NVIDIA and ATI now have their own dual-graphics card technology. The new technology works very differently from 3dfx's analog scan line interleave system, though, which just splits up the screen into several scan lines, each card rendering a line alternately. NVIDIA's system is called "scalable link interface," or SLI. You connect the two cards together with a PCB bridge connector, which offers a choice of rendering modes. The first is SFR (split frame rendering). Here the card splits the screen in two, and a dynamic load balancing system decides what variable portion of the screen goes to which card. In most cases, the bottom of a 3D scene will be more complicated than the sky and, say, the tops of buildings, so giving more power to the bottom two thirds of the screen will give you a faster frame rate than a basic 50/50 split.

The other method is AFR (alternate frame rendering), where each card renders frames alternately.

One major advantage of SLI is that it gives you a future-proof upgrade path, meaning you can buy a PCI-E 6600GT now, and then buy another one later. However, the system is also notoriously fussy, and will even refuse to work with identical cards if one has only a slightly different BIOS. Another issue with SLI is that only a select number of games support it (the official list is available at www.nvzone.com). You can create a driver profile for unsupported games, but there's no guarantee that it will increase performance.

ATI has announced a similar technology called CrossFire. In fact, you might argue that ATI was doing it first anyway, as the company's Rage Fury Maxx was doing Alternate Frame Rendering between two graphics chips back in 1999.

What's more, CrossFire looks set to be the superior technology of the two, adding a further "Image Quality" rendering mode to the SFR and AFR modes, combining the two cards' anti-aliasing patterns to create a super-smooth 10x anti-aliasing pattern that can even be taken up to 12x with a form of super-sampling. Even better, ATI's system allows you to mix and match cards. As long as you have a CrossFire master card (of which there are three variations), you can put in any X800-series PCI-E card and combine the two cards' power. Apparently, NVIDIA is working on a driver version that will let you mix and match cards too, but whether this ever sees the light of day remains to be seen. Finally, CrossFire officially supports every 3D game out there, although again, the performance difference you'll see depends on the game you're running, and whether you're really pushing the settings or not.

Unlike SLI, CrossFire also doesn't require you to fiddle with any connectors on the motherboard or go into your BIOS to turn the dual-GPU 3D graphics mode on and off, as it lets you do all of this through its own software. The only downer about CrossFire is the slightly clunky connection system, requiring a pass-through cable that's reminiscent of the old 3dfx Voodoo 1 and 2 cards.

Of course, to run one of these systems, you'll need a compatible motherboard, and that doesn't just mean any board with two full-size PCI-E slots. VIA's dual-graphics chipsets, for example, still haven't been certified by NVIDIA and won't run SLI. You can, however, get NVIDIA's nForce 4 SLI chipset for both Intel and AMD-based systems. CrossFire, meanwhile, is currently limited to ATI's own Radeon XPress 200P CrossFire Edition chipset.

Whether you need two graphics cards at the moment is up to you. Unless you're upgrading from a 6600GT or an X800, then it's more about show-off value than genuine need. You would have to be running your games at ridiculous settings to see a benefit from two GeForce 7800GTXs. However, it does provide a good upgrade path, so it's worth considering a dual-graphics motherboard now, and then adding another card in a year's time when games become even more complicated, and start using features such as HDR by default.

Left: **Two NVIDIA SLI cards connect together using a PCB bridge connector.**

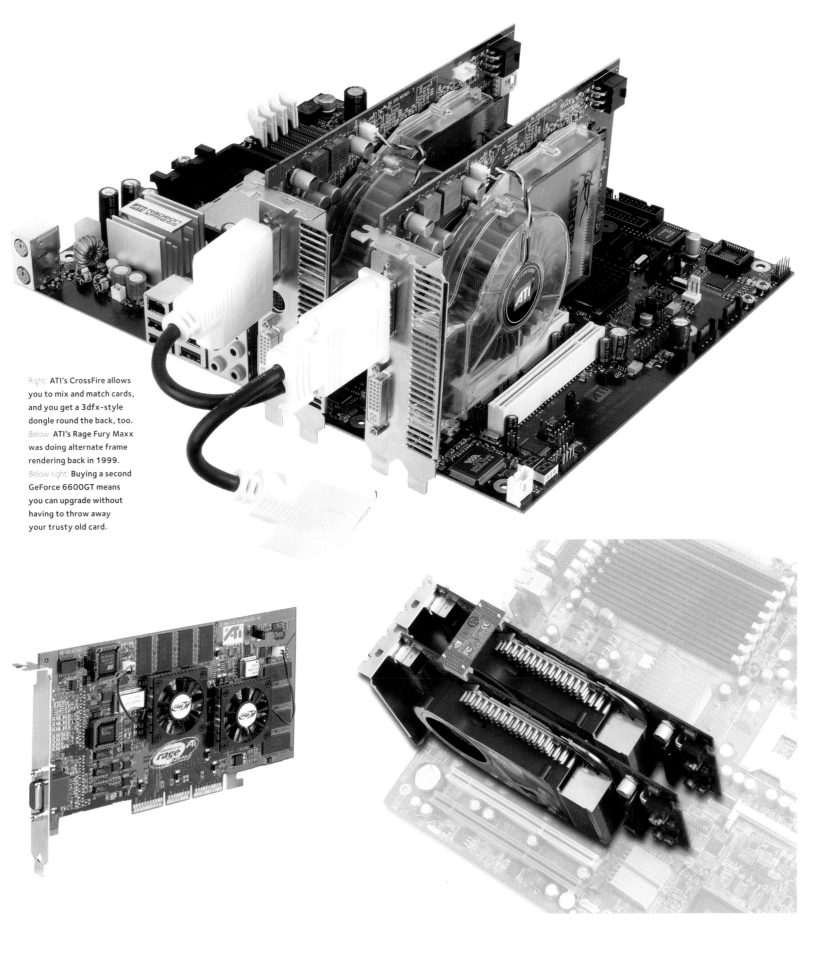

Right: **ATI's CrossFire** allows you to mix and match cards, and you get a 3dfx-style dongle round the back, too.
Below: **ATI's Rage Fury Maxx** was doing alternate frame rendering back in 1999.
Below right: **Buying a second GeForce 6600GT** means you can upgrade without having to throw away your trusty old card.

050 > 051

Monitors

> Some people will tell you that a TFT isn't good enough for gaming, but that's not true.

Considering that it's been around for the best part of a century, it's a wonder that the cathode ray tube (CRT), found in big TVs and monitors worldwide, is still so popular. Used for all sorts of things, from television to radar, it's proved to be an invaluable technology throughout the 20th century. However, the CRT is being rapidly usurped by the slimmer, flatter LCD. No one would have foreseen this from looking at calculators and digital watches twenty years ago, but it's happening. LCD just has too many advantages, particularly in the computer world where pixel-perfect accuracy is demanded.

CRTs still have their place in the PC monitor universe—in professional design and publishing they still lead the way for color accuracy—but for most general purposes a Thin Film Transistor (TFT) is definitely the way to go. They take up far less space and consume less power, there is less room for any sort of geometric distortion in the screen (always a problem with CRT displays), and they don't fill waste dumps with nearly as much lead. In short, if you're buying a new monitor, then buy a TFT.

As you probably know, though, not all TFTs are the same, and there are several things you should be on the look out for before making a purchase. The first is the response time. One strength of CRT technology is that it can cope with constantly updating the screen at 70fps without any blurring between frames. With LCD screens, however, it takes time—admittedly, only milliseconds—for the liquid crystals that make up the pixels to change color. In the early days of TFT panels, this gave the screen a tendency to blur or smear with fast movement: a real problem if you were playing games or watching DVDs.

Fortunately, TFTs have come a long way in the last few years, and you'd need to have incredible vision (not to mention a bizarre perception of time) to notice any blurring between frames on a decent TFT monitor. Some gamers will tell you that a TFT isn't good enough for gaming, but that's not true. Look for a response time of at least 20ms (preferably lower) and your TFT will be able to run games at high frame rates without any blurring.

Another key thing to look for is the viewing angle, the angle from which you can look at the monitor before the picture deteriorates. These are measured both horizontally and vertically and are usually quoted in the specifications, though the measurements are frequently way off. If you look for a few reviews of monitors that mention the viewing angles, then you'll at least have a subjective opinion (which is often the best and most honest type when it comes to monitors) on whether the viewing angles are any good or not.

Size and resolution is also a major factor with monitors. There's no point in having a top of the range graphics card, if its performance is going to be CPU-limited on your 15in 1,024 x 768 monitor. If you're

Right: **Most graphics cards come with a DVI output these days, so it's worth getting a monitor that will use it.**

Left: **There's no point in building a high end system if you're going to plug it into a 15in monitor.**

building a high-spec gaming system, then it needs a high-spec monitor, it's as simple as that. A bigger monitor doesn't necessarily equate to a higher resolution, though. 19in TFTs are a good case in point, as they often have a resolution of 1,280 x 1,024, which is exactly the same number of pixels that you'll get on a 17in TFT. Some argue that, this being the case, it's not worth "wasting" the extra money. I'd argue that it is. After all, you'll be able to look at the screen from further away, which will be kinder to your eyes, and it will also give your games a bigger screen area, even if the resolution isn't any higher.

Finally, the other thing worth looking for on a monitor is a DVI (digital video interface) input. Just about every graphics card worth its salt will have a DVI port (and sometimes two), and connecting it straight to a DVI monitor will cut out any analog interference and noise. This is worth paying for.

Remember that your monitor is likely to last several years longer than your PC, and will probably survive several entire PC upgrades, so make sure you get a decent one. It's better to spend a bit more money on your monitor and a bit less on your processor or graphics card if you have to—it's a good long-term investment.

Right: **Look for a display with a fast response time, a DVI input, and a native resolution of 1,280 x 1,024. This 17in Sharp has all of the above.**

052 > 053

Speaker types

> Unless you have the space to set up a mini IMAX in your living room, your best bet is to get a decent 2.1 or 5.1 speaker set.

A few years ago, surround sound belonged purely in the domain of multiplex cinemas and overpaid people who could afford the necessary space and equipment to create a "home theater" system. That time has thankfully passed, and now even entry-level PCs have the ability to output surround sound. However, there are still plenty of confusing standards when it comes to choosing your speakers.

Know your sound systems:

Stereo: Two speakers, each with its own independent channel. Simple.

2.1: Stereo speakers with a subwoofer to handle the bass frequencies. Small computer desktop speakers often sound pretty weedy, but having the subwoofer can give a real lift to the bass. Unfortunately, these sets tend to lack mid-range frequencies.

Dolby Pro Logic: A kind of quasi-surround sound, where a stereo signal is spread over several speakers, instead of each speaker being connected to its own independent channel.

Dolby Digital 5.1: The most common surround sound standard simply involves a subwoofer, one front center speaker, two front stereo speakers, and two stereo rear speakers. This is more than enough for a basic living room surround sound system without going into overkill.

Dolby Digital EX: A surround sound system with either six or seven channels, and a subwoofer. This involves a front center speaker, two front stereo speakers, two rear stereo speakers, and a further two speakers (or sometimes one) directly behind the listener. This is the same as THX EX.

THX: An acronym that comes from George Lucas' film project *THX118*. On its own THX actually means nothing in terms of surround sound, except that the sound system has been approved by THX (www.thx.com).

THX EX: A Dolby Digital EX system that's been approved by THX.

DTS: Despite what you might think, the "D" in DTS doesn't actually stand for "Dolby." DTS is a different standard in its own right, involving a 5.1 surround sound system similar to Dolby Digital, offering a higher bit rate of 1.536Mbits per second (Dolby Digital is limited to a maximum of 448Kbits per second). This doesn't guarantee better quality, but it makes it possible, though Dolby Digital remains very much the mainstream standard.

Every basic sound card available today will have the outputs to connect directly to a 5.1 surround system without a decoder, and many even go as far as 7.1 surround sound. In fact, even most integrated audio setups on motherboards will quite happily do one or both, as well.

Unless you have the space to set up a mini IMAX in your living room, your best bet is to either get a decent 2.1 or 5.1 speaker set. These will be great for DVD movies, and many games also use 5.1 sound, which makes the experience all the more believable.

Bear in mind, though, that finding space for all these little boxes (not to mention their wiring) can be a major headache. Surround sound is great, but it requires space, so think about what you really want from your PC. There's no point in cluttering up your lounge with stuff you don't need just because your PC has the capability to produce surround sound. Many people find that it's better to purchase a decent set of stereo speakers than spend the same amount on a 5.1 surround set, so if you're short on space and aren't planning to watch DVD movies on your PC, then this is a much more practical route to take.

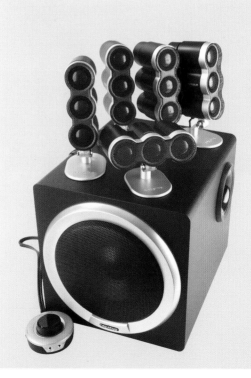

Left: **There are lots of standards in surround sound, but they're not always as important as they look.**

Right: **Creative's Sound Blaster Audigy 2 sound card is compatible with just about every surround standard out there—it's even THX-certified!**
Left: **The happy compromise: A set of 5.1 speakers is easier to find room for, and it's compatible with Dolby Digital and DTS too.**

Above: **If you have space, then why not go for the ultimate surround sound experience. This set of Creative 7.1 speakers will let you run Dolby Digital EX surround sound in all its glory.**
Left: **Ask yourself what you need before you cover your lounge in wires. A decent set of stereo speakers, such as Creative's MegaWorks 2.1 set, will still sound fine and you won't need to find space for them.**

054 > 055

Keyboards and mice

> There's no point in having a beautiful silver PC if it's got a monstrous beige keyboard and mouse plugged into it.

Often overlooked as the boring "bread and butter" parts of the PC, the faithful keyboard and mouse should actually be up there with your CPU and graphics card as top priorities. Every time you use your computer, you will have to use a keyboard and mouse, and you don't want this to be a chore. These too will transfer from one machine to another without the need for constant upgrading, so like monitors, keyboards and mice are an investment, so don't just plump for the cheap and cheerful option.

You don't just want to buy the keyboard and mouse that offer the most comfort and the best features, either. Let's face it, there's no point in having a beautiful silver PC if it's got a monstrous beige keyboard and mouse plugged into it. Still, finding a balance between the two can prove difficult.

In terms of quirky looks, the Eluminix illuminated keyboard certainly stands out, and it will also complement a PC that features blue cold cathode lights. The Sinclair Spectrum-esque rubbery keys do take a lot of getting used to, becoming quite uncomfortable after long periods.

Another case in point is Cooler Master's Q Alloy Keyboard, which has a classy, solid metal case that will look just right next to a silver PC. Once again, though, the keys aren't nearly as comfortable to use as those on a normal keyboard. It's a bit like typing on a really big laptop, with shallow key presses.

If you're on a budget, then another good way to get a good looking, well-built keyboard, is to look on eBay for second hand keyboards from old business PCs. HP, Compaq, Dell, and IBM have made a great selection of silver and black keyboards for their business PCs over the years, and you can often pick these up second hand.

You can also apply this to mice—there are plenty of black Dell (rebadged Microsoft) mice that will do the job perfectly. However, there are other considerations to think of with mice. If you just want to use Windows and play occasional games then a standard two-button mouse is fine. If you're really into gaming, though, then a gaming mouse with plenty of assignable buttons will make first person shooters and real time strategy games much easier. Logitech make some great gaming mice, such as the MX510, which are well worth a look.

Your best bet is to go for a keyboard and mouse set made by a company with decades of experience in designing them. The latest keyboard and mouse sets from the likes of Microsoft and Logitech are not only well built and ergonomic, but they also look fairly classy. Microsoft's Wireless Optical Desktop Elite is a fine example, and Logitech's Di Novo Media Desktop, while extremely expensive, looks and feels absolutely awesome.

One word of warning when buying wireless keyboard and mouse sets—Bluetooth wireless sets can often be a real nightmare. If they work, they're fine. However, they often lose their connections, and can sometimes take quite a while to get working again, which can make you want to throw your Bluetooth mouse out of the window if you're working on something urgent. The old-school RF wireless sets are generally more reliable, but they also have a limited range. This might affect you if you build a PC for your living room, but it won't if they are just sitting on a desk next to your computer. It seems there is no substitute for good old fashioned wires when it comes to reliability.

Left: **An old Compaq keyboard from eBay will be cheap, well-built and the right color to have next to your silver or black PC.**

Opposite, clockwise from top:
Logitech Di Novo Media Desktop.
The Eluminix keyboard has a distinctive look, but it's not that comfortable to type on after a while.
Logitech MX510 Game Mouse—a mouse with lots of buttons will make gaming much easier.

Cooler Master Q Alloy Keyboard.
Microsoft Wireless Optical Desktop Elite.

Cooling

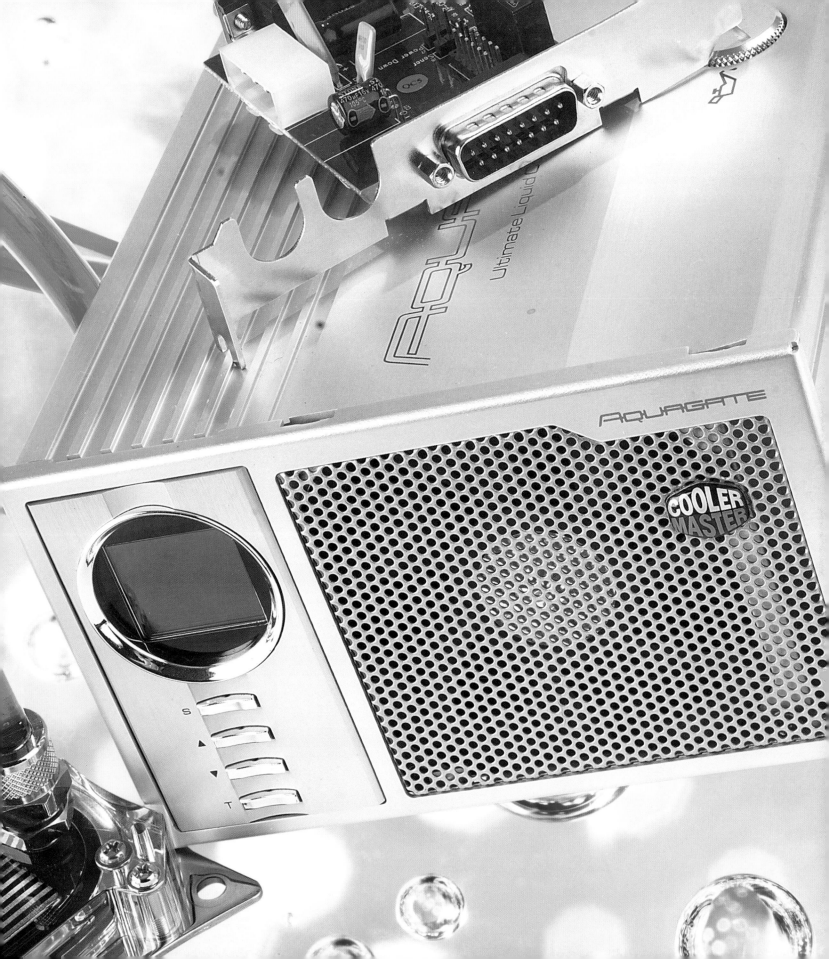

058 > 059

Keep your cool

> Your PC has to be cooled efficiently. This will prevent it from locking up, and extend the life of your components.

If you were the unfortunate demonic minion that Satan assigned to work in Hell's boiler room, storing the hot towels for sizzling swimmers emerging from the lake of fire, then you'd have a fair idea of what it feels like to be one of today's PC components. Heat is your system's arch enemy, and a whole sub-industry has sprung up specifically to combat it.

Cooling your PC is now a science in itself, and there are various ways of doing it, from passive heatsinks, to fans, through liquid cooling and then into the realms of phase change cooling. It's hard to imagine now, but 12 years ago you didn't need any cooling for your components; a CPU was a bare chip and the only noise would have come from the fan on your power supply.

Cooling just wasn't needed for chips back then, but it's been gradually encroaching on your PC's innards ever since, starting with simple passive heatsinks on the later 486s and slowly progressing into the monstrous heatsink and fan assemblies that you see on today's processors and graphics cards. Cooling is absolutely essential for PC components now, and your PC would lock up within seconds if you forgot to plug in the fan on your processor.

The reason for this is largely due to Moore's Law—a theory devised by Intel's Gordon Moore that predicted that the number of transistors on a silicon integrated circuit would double every 18 months. This has pretty much held true until now, and with so many transistors getting packed into such a small space, it's inevitable that more and more heat is produced.

Cooling is a problem with PCs today, but it can be used to your advantage if you twist it in the right ways. Exceed the basic cooling requirements of your chip, and you can overclock it even further; with a liquid cooling system you should be able to overclock it to a ridiculous level. On the other end of the scale, if you're not interested in making your PC faster, you can certainly cut down on the amount of noise that your PC produces by fitting quieter alternative coolers to your CPU and graphics card.

Either way, your PC still has to be cooled efficiently, as this will prevent it from locking up, and extend the life of your components. Many factors can affect this, including the size of your fans, which direction they point in, and where you position your components and cabling.

Of course, we can't condense the theories of cooling that companies have invested years of research into over just a couple of pages, but we can show you the basics that you'll need to create an efficiently cooled PC that's both quiet and overclockable.

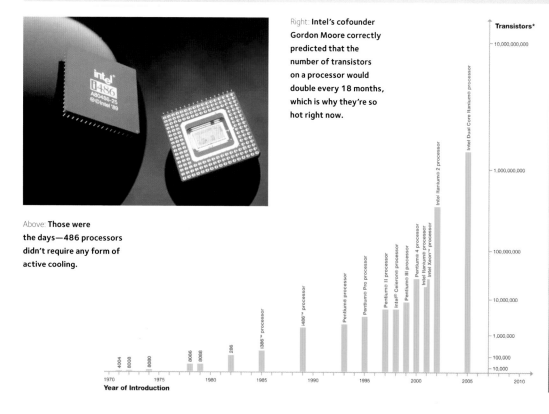

Above: **Those were the days—486 processors didn't require any form of active cooling.**

Right: **Intel's cofounder Gordon Moore correctly predicted that the number of transistors on a processor would double every 18 months, which is why they're so hot right now.**

Moore's Law

In 1965, Intel co-founder Gordon Moore predicted that the number of transistors on a piece of silicon would double every couple of years—an insight later dubbed "Moore's Law." His prediction has held true, as ever-shrinking transistor sizes have allowed exponential growth in the number of transistors on a single chip.

Moore's Law is now a be... tronics industry, and intel applies its principles li... Whole new ways for people to play, lear... have come about as the company has ... re's Law.

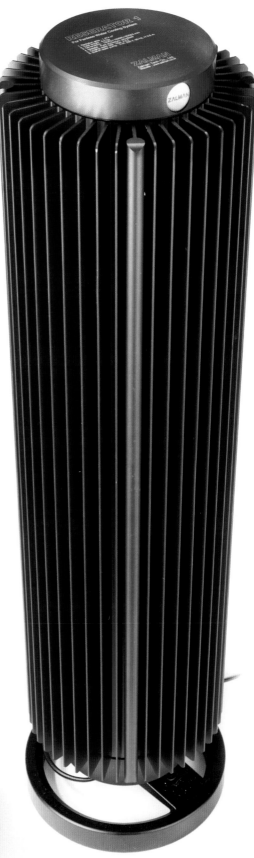

Above: **The pure copper version of Zalman's "flower" cooler costs more than the aluminum and copper hybrid because of its higher thermal conductivity.**

Right: **Today's PCs need small jet engines or props from Ed Wood movies to cool them, but there are tricks to getting a good balance.**

060 > 061

Air cooling

> The purpose of your case fan is to cool the PC down as a whole, so that the airflow covers as much of the motherboard as possible.

The first, and most important, rule when it comes to setting up fans is the direction of your airflow. You might think that attaching a fan to every single bracket in your case and pointing them toward the processor will make things cooler, but what it will actually do is keep the same stale, hot air circulating in your case for much longer than you want it there.

The way around this is simple—you need to make sure that all the air inside your case has a definite direction from the start to finish. Basically, the air needs to come in from one end of your PC, and then out of the other. Ideally, you want the air to be coming in through the front of your case and going out the back, but you can get away with doing it the other way around too.

As you probably know, there are two sides of a fan—the side that pushes air forward, and the side that sucks air in. With this in mind, you want the fans at the front of your PC positioned so that they're sucking air from the outside through the intake vents at the front of your case, blowing the cool air over the motherboard. You then need to reverse the process with the fans at the back, so that they're positioned facing outward, to suck the hot air from inside the PC. Naturally enough, these rear fans are known as "exhaust" fans, and you can buy ones specifically for the job that have their power connectors on the right side, as well as exhaust blowers that fit into a PCI slot and push air out through a vent in the back.

Don't worry about your CPU and GPU fans, though, as they will have a small, specific job of blowing a certain amount of concentrated air on to their assigned chips, so they won't cause havoc with your airflow system. However, your case fans can certainly help to push the air dispersed from these fans in the right direction (out the back) if they're positioned correctly.

The purpose of your case fan is to cool the PC down as a whole, so that the airflow covers as much of the motherboard as possible before it's vented outside. Just to be sure, you can also put some ducting around the fans to ensure that the airflow goes in exactly the right direction.

You need to apply this same principle to any modding projects too, and it's really very simple. Just ensure that you've drilled some intake and exhaust holes on either side, and position your fans accordingly.

If you don't have a directional airflow system in your PC, then you'll get "negative airflow" where multiple streams of airflow collide and end up not going anywhere. This is a recipe for disaster, as you will want to keep the air moving in order to keep your components cool.

With all this in mind, it's important to check for the available fan mounts on a case, as well as their ventilation holes, before making a purchase. Some cases are very badly designed and don't even have intake vents on the front, while some come with everything you need already in position.

Above: **This exhaust fan takes up a PCI slot and disperses the hot air from your PC through a vent at the back.**
Right: **Just turn your fan the other way around to turn it into an exhaust fan.**

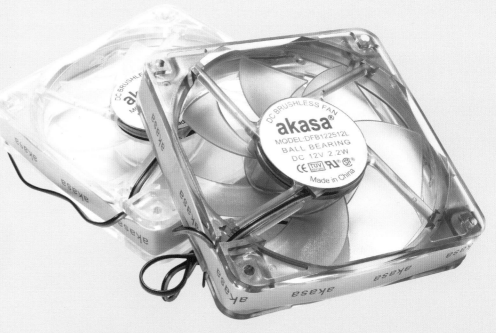

Right: **Your CPU fan will focus its airflow on to the CPU, but you can help shift the resulting hot air with a decent case airflow system.**

062 > 063

Cooling principles

> Your heatsink's primary job is to take heat away from the chip, and it can only do this if the material it's made from is an efficient thermal conductor.

There are many other factors to bear in mind when choosing the correct cooling method for your components. When it comes to cooling specific parts of your PC, such as your CPU and graphics card, the fan will also be attached to a heatsink (known as an HSF—heatsink fan), which is there to help shift as much heat away from the chip in the shortest amount of time. With this in mind, you need to make sure that the HSFs you buy are up to the job of cooling your components, which you can do by finding out their thermal design power (TDP).

The TDP is basically the amount of heat energy (in watts) that needs to be removed from a component in order for it to function correctly. This information is usually fairly easy to find with some quick research on the Web, and if you can track down the TDP for your component, you can then add the most suitable HSF. Intel's latest chips have a particularly high TDP (often way in excess of 100W), which is why they need a lot more in the way of cooling than AMD's chips. You also need to bear in mind that overclocking these components will push the TDP even higher, so overclockers need to install coolers that can remove well over and above the required TDP. The TDP is like a worst-case scenario, and your chip will be producing less energy most of the time, but you need to make sure that you have the required cooling headroom for the occasions when your PC is running at full tilt.

So, what makes a powerful cooler? You can generally apply the rule that bigger is better. There are many sizes available—with their diameters usually measured in millimeters—but the usual ones are 80mm and 120mm models, with occasional 60mm fans for specific applications. You want to get the biggest fans possible, basically because bigger fans can push out more air with less work, meaning that they not only create more cool air, but they can also do it at a lower spin speed, meaning they'll be that much quieter. Along similar lines, a smaller fan with deeper and thicker blades, as found on Arctic Cooling's Freezer CPU models will also be quiet and effective when accompanied by an effective heatsink.

It's often a secondary consideration, but the design of the heatsink is only as good as the materials used to construct it. Your heatsink's primary job is to take as much heat away from the chip as quickly as possible, and it can only do this if the material it's made from is an efficient thermal conductor. There's actually a huge difference in the thermal conductivity of various materials, with mercury conducting virtually no heat at all, and diamonds removing all the heat in no time. Somewhere in the middle you'll find the most common heatsink materials; aluminum and copper. Copper is almost twice as thermally conductive as aluminum—and silver is more conductive than both of them if you can find it—which is why you pay more for Zalman's pure copper CNPS7700-CU CPU cooler than you do for the copper and aluminum hybrid.

This rule also applies to waterblocks in water-cooling systems. Again, you want as much heat removed from the processor and passed to the water cooler as possible, and you want it done quickly. This is why you sometimes see a big copper block on the base of waterblocks too, although gold is also commonly used as it doesn't corrode so easily if in direct contact with water.

Right: The base on this WaterChill CPU cooler will transfer the CPU's heat quickly to the circulating coolant.

Above: **Deeper and thicker blades will make a fan more effective and often quieter.**

Far right: **Heatsinks often have a copper base to move the heat through the heatsink as quickly as possible.**

Right: **The latest Pentium Extreme Edition chips have a TDP well in excess of 100W, and will need a hefty cooler to take the heat from them.**

064 > 065

TIM

> Thermal adhesive is great stuff, but don't ever use it to stick a heatsink to a CPU. It will never come off.

TIM stands for "thermal interface material," and it's basically the gunk that sits between a chip (be it a CPU, GPU, or Northbridge) and the heatsink (or waterblock) that it's attached to.

So why do you need it? After all, heatsinks are made of metal (one of the best heat conductors available), and CPUs usually have a metal heat spreader attached to them, too. Why do you need anything else? Well, that should be enough in theory, but it relies on both your heatsink and your CPU's heat spreader having completely flat surfaces to ensure that all of the heat is transferred efficiently. Unfortunately, though, completely flat heatsinks are about as common as polar bears in Texas. With just the two bits of metal touching, you're not going to shift as much heat as you need.

This is where TIM comes in; filling in all the gaps to ensure that there is a larger surface area to transfer the heat, and that as much heat is translated from the chip to the heatsink as possible. TIM is cheap, even for the top quality stuff, such as Arctic Silver 5, so there's no excuse not to use it.

The first job is to prime the heatsink, so put a splodge of TIM on the part of the heatsink that will touch the chip, and then cover one of your index fingers with something protective (a pair of latex gloves will do the job) and rub the TIM over the heatsink's contact area. This will stop any bits of skin getting into the mix—you don't want any stray materials getting in the way, as

they will just render all of your hard work pointless. For this same reason, you will also want to rub off the excess with a lint-free cloth.

Once you've done that, the next step is to squeeze a tiny amount of TIM onto the middle of your chip, and plop the heatsink on top of this, then rub it about a bit to spread the TIM as evenly as possible.

When applying a new coat, perhaps if you're upgrading your CPU, you should remove any TIM from both the chip and heatsink. A great tool for this is Akasa's TIM cleaner, and a bottle will last a lifetime unless you're a serial upgrader. You don't need much of it, just drip a little bit on to a lint-free cloth and you should be able to remove the gunk. It's also worth doing this to remove the worthless little squares of TIM that you get with Intel's stock heatsinks, so that you can then apply sufficient TIM to cover the whole CPU's heat spreader, rather than just a small part of it.

One thing to note is that TIM isn't glue; you'll still be able to remove the heatsink from your chip with a bit of wrestling. However, there are also some forms of thermal adhesive, heat conducting glue that not only sticks the heatsink to the chip, but also ensures that it still transfers heat. One example of this is Arctic Alumina Thermal Adhesive. This stuff is great for getting difficult heatsinks to stick onto graphics cards that don't have the right pin-mounts, but it will never, ever come unstuck, so don't stick it to a CPU. Ever. Believe me, I speak from painful experience...

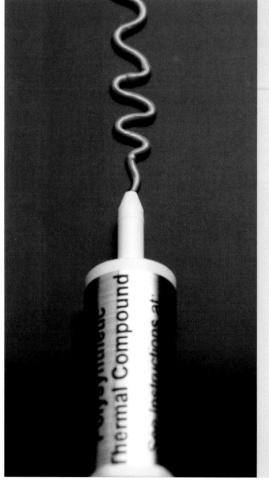

Left: **If you get bored, you can always use your TIM syringe to make some arty photography.**

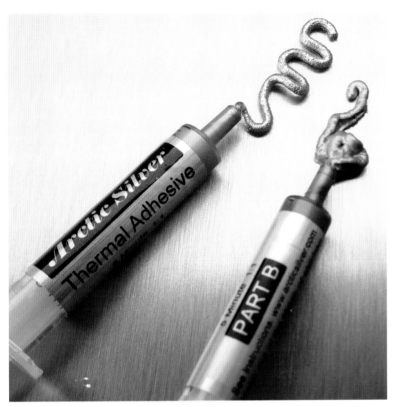

Above: **Arctic Silver's two-part thermal adhesive lets you glue a heatsink directly to a chip, which can be useful for adding a heatsink to your Northbridge.**

Right: **...but don't use it to stick an expensive CPU to a heatsink.**

Below: **Akasa's TIM Cleaner is really handy, and you'll get enough in the bottle to clean the slime off CPUs for a lifetime.**

066 > 067

Water of life

> Some crazies build their own water cooling systems from tropical fish pumps, but the easiest way is to buy a ready-made kit.

People often say that they can't understand why you would risk water cooling your PC—surely mixing water with electronics is a pretty bad idea? Believe it or not, though, water cooling very rarely results in computers going out in a fireworks display, and if they do, it'll be because they haven't been installed properly.

For a start, you can cut down the electrical conductivity of your water (or coolant, as it's pretentiously called by the industry) by using deionized water (readily available from any hardware store), which has the ions removed and, in theory, shouldn't be able to conduct electricity at all. In practice, it can sometimes become conductive again after a while, but this really isn't something you need to worry about.

Another (and more popular) alternative is to buy some distilled water, which is free from minerals. This stops it from clogging up your cooling system with limescale, and can also stop your parts from corroding. Mix this with an additive to reduce algae growth in your loop, a bottle of which is often supplied with kits. Another route is to add a perfluorocarbon (although this is expensive stuff) to make your water inert and stop it conducting, as well as dramatically lowering the water's freezing point. Opinion is divided on which course to take, but either way is unquestionably better than straight tap water. You can also get a variety of colored additives to make your tubing look great too.

So what makes up a water cooling kit? Well, some crazies build their own water cooling systems from scratch, using a variety of parts from car radiators and tropical fish pumps, but the easiest way (by far) is to do it with a ready-made water cooling kit. The basic idea is to create a loop of water which is pumped via tubes through a cooling radiator, and then through some waterblocks, which replace the heatsinks on your hottest components: the CPU, GPU, and the Northbridge chip. The idea is that a high flow of water

running over the waterblock will move the heat from the component to the water. With a more powerful pump and more inlets on your waterblocks, even more water will be moved to the radiator, and the whole water cooling loop will become even cooler. There's normally a reservoir in the loop, too, that provides an easy-access filling point, and helps to prevent troublesome air bubbles entering the system.

The setup you should go for really depends on your priorities (see page 70). You can also mix and match ready-made components to get the system that suits you best. One major thing to bear in mind, though, is that you'll need somewhere to put it all, so measure up your case before getting started. Parts such as pumps, and even reservoirs, are usually easy to house, but a large radiator can be harder to install. Many sizes of radiator are available, and they're usually measured in terms of how many fans they can accommodate and what size they are. As you can imagine, a three 120mm fan radiator is going to require some serious modding to your case if you're going to fit it inside.

You will also need to buy tubing of the appropriate diameter for your parts, but this gets tricky. Some stores measure by the outer diameter, and others by the inner diameter. There are basically two main tubing outer-diameter sizes—1/2in for loops with a high flow rate (which are cooler and better for overclocking), and 3/8in tubing for low flow rate setups (which are quieter). To make things slightly more complicated, there are also two main types of connector—the barb, which is just a plastic plug with a barb on the end that attaches to the cable, and the push-fit connector, where you have to feed the tubing through a hole until it hits an "O-ring" and locks. Of course, if you buy a ready-made kit then you don't have to worry about any of this.

Right: **Use an additive with your distilled water to prevent corrosion, and to give it a bit of color.**

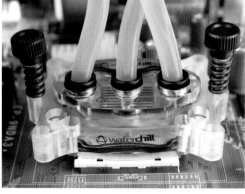

Above: **WaterChill Kit.**
A reservoir (top right) makes
the system easy to fill, and
also helps to trap air bubbles.
Left: **Waterblocks are
attached to hot components
such as the CPU and GPU,
where they take over the
job of the heatsink.**
Far left: **The radiator cools the
water in the loop, and they
come in a variety of sizes.**

068 > 069

Different setups

> The problem with the Reserator is that its passive cooling system simply can't shift as much heat as fan-assisted setups.

If you're new to water cooling, then the best place to start is with a simple kit that comes with all the parts you need. One perfect beginner kit is the Cool River, available in both 80mm and 120mm versions, and comes with waterblocks for your CPU, GPU, and Northbridge. What's more, it also comes with a pre-filled, sealed reservoir, so all you have to do is connect it all up and set it off.

The next step up is something from Asetek's excellent WaterChill range (www.asetek.com), which offers various kits and separate components to build the loop that's most appropriate for your system. Asetek offers a powerful and flexible range of water cooling parts (there's even a waterblock for your hard drive!), and the supplied documentation is also pretty good. With this equipment you should be able to get up and running with no problems—though it helps if you take your time.

There are also plenty of other respectable water cooling kits on the market, including Cooler Master's Aquagate, which can take the place of a second PSU if you have a big enough case. Meanwhile, Corsair's Cool kit is also worth a look, coming with a 120mm radiator and plenty of overclocking headroom. Then, at the top of the heap you'll find kits such as the Koolance Exos, a ludicrous four fan system that allows you to overclock a dual Xeon system.

Another popular kit, meanwhile, is the Zalman Reserator, which is a very different beast from the usual setups. It's designed to make the cooling system as quiet as possible, rather than provide maximum overclocking

headroom. It's basically a huge passive radiator (which also acts as a reservoir) without any fans, and it uses the principle of convection to shift the heat to the top if its tower, while your PC's water supply comes from the cool water at the bottom. The kit comes with a CPU water block as standard, although there are also GPU and Northbridge waterblocks available. The Reserator makes no more noise than a humming fish tank (in fact, it's actually a bit quieter).

The only downer with the Reserator is that its passive cooling system simply can't shift as much heat as fan-assisted systems. This means you need to total up the TDP of all the components you're going to cool before you start, and be careful. There is sufficient potential to cool an Athlon 64 4000+ and a GeForce 6600GT with it, but a dual-core Pentium and a 6800 would be asking too much.

Of course, once you've become experienced in the ways of water cooling, you can start to branch out, putting together your own customized system using the parts of your choice. Water cooling is big business now, and sites such as www.frozencpu.com, www.cooltechnica.com, or www.componentsuk.co.uk are dedicated to providing the exact system you want. For example, Danger Den produces a superb range of waterblocks, and an AngelEye reservoir will look fantastic in a 5.25in drive bay. Once you've built up some experience and know what you want, you'll be able to design and install a custom water cooling loop that fits your requirements perfectly.

Left & Right: **Cooler Master and Corsair offer some great water cooling kits.**

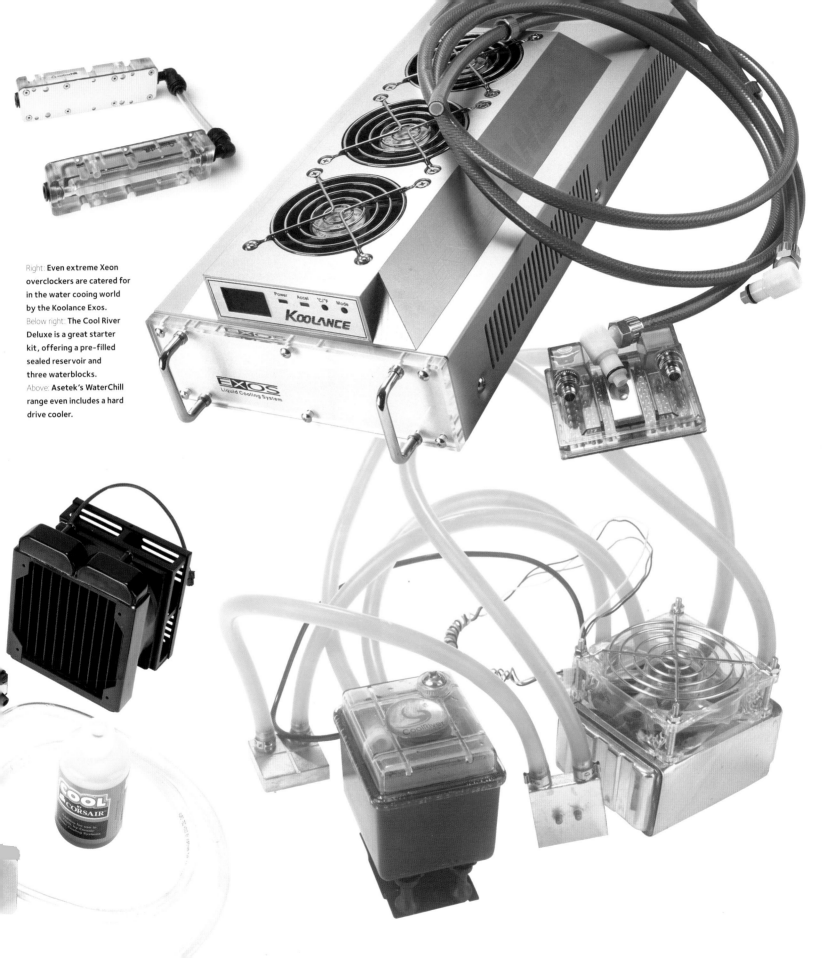

Right: **Even extreme Xeon overclockers are catered for in the water cooing world by the Koolance Exos.**
Below right: **The Cool River Deluxe is a great starter kit, offering a pre-filled sealed reservoir and three waterblocks.**
Above: **Asetek's WaterChill range even includes a hard drive cooler.**

Setting up water cooling

> Connect the water cooling kit on your work surface first to make sure everything connects correctly and doesn't leak.

Once you've got all your pieces, you'll want to make absolutely sure that you install them correctly the first time or you could be looking at giving your computer a shower. Correct additives or not, this is something that you'll want to avoid.

With this in mind, there are a few guidelines to follow when installing your water cooling loop, not just to keep your system safe, but to also make it as efficient as possible. Your first job before you start filling up the reservoir is to put the kit inside your PC, making sure that everything fits, and also measuring up the exact lengths of tubing you'll need. Make absolutely sure that there are no kinks in your tubing while you're here, keeping in mind that you can get splitters to make your tubing turn sharp corners (the guys who sold you your water cooling system will have them). You do, however, want to keep these bits and pieces to a minimum, as the more bends there are in your system, the less efficiently your pump will be circulating the water.

It's also worth noting a few general rules for where you should place components. Your reservoir, for example, should ideally be placed above the rest of the component loop (this includes the Zalman Reserator), as this will help it trap any rising hot air before it gets into the pump. You will also want your radiator to be positioned somewhere that will get plenty of airflow. Accordingly, your radiator should be placed so that its fan is sucking air from outside the case and passing it

over the radiator. This is why you'll see many water-cooled systems with the radiator unit fixed to the outside of the case. You can mount it inside the case if you position the fan correctly, but this will inevitably mean that your loop won't be as cool.

Once you've worked out where everything is going, remove the kit and link it all up on its own on your work surface, following the instructions to make sure everything in the loop is in the right order, and that the tubing is connected to the right end of each part (each one will have an inlet and an outlet, or sometimes two inlets instead—you don't want to mix them up). Once you're sure that everything is correctly in place, you can fill the reservoir and start the pump. If it all goes round smoothly with no bubbles, no funny noises, and no pool of water appearing underneath it, then you can safely move it all back into your case again (making sure that you've filled your reservoir with some additive-enhanced distilled water first).

Then, once everything is in place, start the pump (before turning the computer on) just to make sure that there still aren't any problems. If you see any water leaking out, don't panic—just remove the kit and the wet components and leave them to dry—they'll be fine once the water's gone. When you're satisfied that everything is working, you can then switch on your PC and enjoy the silence, or at least some extra headroom for overclocking.

Left: **Make sure you connect your tubing to the correct inlets and outlets on all of your components.**

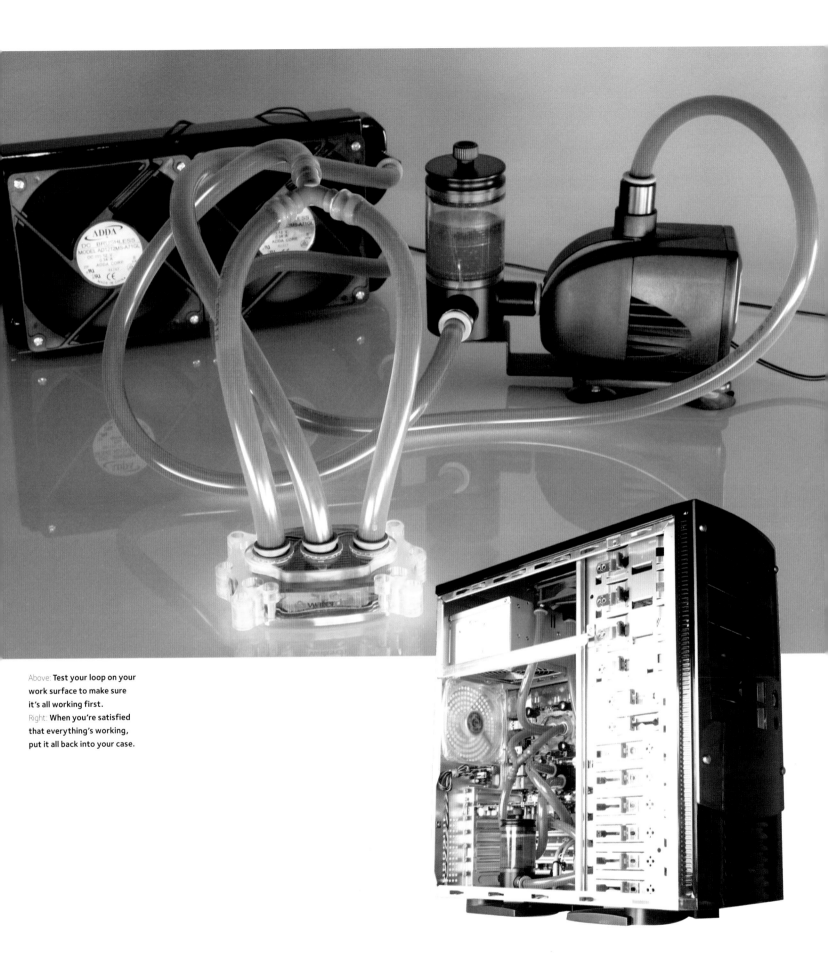

Above: **Test your loop on your work surface to make sure it's all working first.**
Right: **When you're satisfied that everything's working, put it all back into your case.**

The next phase

> Phase change coolers are undoubtedly the best thing out there for overclocking. They can remove up to 200W of heat energy from a CPU.

Using fans and water to cool down your components is fairly obvious, but the next step is to take it to the extreme, especially if you want to overclock your parts that little bit further. If you have plenty of money, and want to build what could end up being among the fastest PCs in the world, then you need to get into the realms of extreme cooling.

One way of doing this is with thermoelectric converters (TECs). These work on the principle of the Peltier effect, discovered by the French physicist Jean Peltier in 1834. The basic idea is that by passing an electrical current through two dissimilar metals that are connected to each other at two points, the current will drive the heat from one junction to another.

The upshot of this is that the metal at one junction gets incredibly hot, while the other gets very cold. It's the latter that you want right next to your chip and you then need some way to pull the heat off the hot side of the TEC, which usually means a hefty waterblock with a couple of inlets and a high-flow pump to shift as much heat as possible. TECs and the bits to connect them are now readily available from most specialist overclocking stores.

Setting up a TEC-based cooling system isn't necessarily difficult, but you do want to make absolutely sure that you have it wired up the right way around; a simple change in polarity will mean that the hot side of the TEC is next to your chip, and will fry it in the process.

Still not cool enough? Your next step is a phase change cooler, which is really a pretentious way of saying "a refrigeration unit in your PC." As its name suggests, this method of cooling is based on the principle of changing a liquid into a gas or vapor—absorbing the heat—then changing it back to a liquid, which can release it. The process does, however, require a huge refrigeration system, which will require a lot of attention to connect up properly.

There are two ways of setting up a ready-made phase change cooler—one is to buy the cooler and connect it up to the PC in your own case; the other is to buy a ready-made case with the cooler already in it. One example of the latter is Asetek's (www.asetek.com) range of curvy VapoChill cases.

Phase change coolers are undoubtedly the best thing out there for CPU overclocking. They can reach Arctic temperatures, and remove up to 200W of heat energy from a CPU. However, you can only cool one component with that massive refrigeration system, which means it's for CPU cooling only. Accordingly, this means that you'll have to find alternative ways to cool your graphics card and Northbridge. Some companies, such as Real Machines (see page 140), will, however, take all the hassle out of it for you by providing a ready-built VapoChill system with a water cooling loop to take care of the rest of the components. The only problem is that you have to pay for it, and at around $6,000, they certainly ain't cheap.

Left: **Asetek's VapoChill LightSpeed can remove up to 200W from a CPU, and can be attached to the bottom of an aluminium case.**

Below: **Phase change coolers can reach Arctic temperatures.**
Top Right: **It's like a refrigeration unit, but it's in your PC.**
Right: **Phase change coolers can take your CPU well below zero, but you'll need another way to remove the heat from the rest of your components.**

Seen and heard

076 › 077

Silence of the fans

> A good way to reduce noise is to use larger fans. The bigger blades rotate slower, making less sound.

As we've already established, modern computer components get hotter than a lake of fire in the afterlife, which also means that they require heatsinks and fans the size of bricks, that make your PC sound like a wind farm. This can be incredibly annoying if you're trying to work or watch a DVD, or even if you're really trying to concentrate in a game. Thankfully, this isn't a noise that you have to put up with, and there are actually several ways to make peace with your PC.

One good way to get the noise down is to simply use larger fans. This might sound like fool's logic, but with bigger blades a larger fan can not only push out more air than a smaller fan, but it can also do it at a slower rotational speed, which means less of the usual high-pitched screaming associated with smaller fans.

Look at the fan mountings in your case and measure them up. If your case has room to replace any of the 80mm fans with 120mm units then this is a good step. However, it's also worth paying for decent quality fans. It's no good, for example, if your fan is bigger but still has a noisy bearing creating a constant rattle. Speaking of which, you can cut down any vibration from your fans with a silicone mount, such as the AcoustiFan range.

You will also need a fan controller to keep the noise in check, and if you've got room in your case it's a good idea to get one that fits into an external-facing drive bay for easy access. Then, you just need to connect your fans to the back of it, and turn the wailing hiss down if you're trying to concentrate, and up if you want to increase your benchmark scores.

Silencing PCs has become a whole industry in itself these days, and plenty of companies have come up with other ideas, one of which is Akasa's Paxmate (www.akasa.co.uk). This is a type of soundproof matting that you line the outside of your case with to block the noise. However, while this can help to muffle annoying high-pitched noises, I've found that it doesn't help a lot with reducing the overall volume.

It is, however, very cheap, and still worth trying out if your PC is really noisy. If you use Paxmate, or any other type of noise-dampening material such as the type found in the AcoustiPack kits from www.quietpc.com, then be very careful where you stick it. Your case will have been designed with ventilation holes in specific places, and if you cover these with matting you're going to mess up your airflow, negating all the good work done by your fans.

Of course, the best way to eliminate noise is to eliminate fans altogether, and several companies have tried to offer ways of doing this. As previously mentioned, Zalman's Reserator can cool your CPU and lower-spec GPU without any fans at all. Not only that, but it also looks like a piece of scenery from the film *Metropolis*, and will look great next to your PC. These cost around $250, and will make two of the noisiest fans in your PC redundant, meaning that you just need a quiet power supply to make a half-decent quiet PC. ThermalTake has just launched a very similar cooler called the Rocket, which also uses a passive radiator to cool the water as quietly possible.

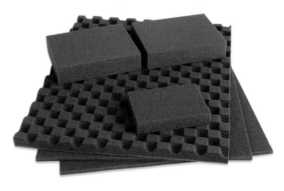

Left: **Bigger fans can push more air at a slower speed, the lower pitch will mean less noise.**
Right: **Sound dampening materials won't cut out all the noise, but they can help to wipe out the really annoying high-pitched whines.**

Above: **Visit a specialist store and pick up some silicone mounts for your fans to stop them vibrating.**

Below: **A front-mounted fan controller is great for controlling the noise of your fans. Turn them up for games, and then turn them down when you're trying to concentrate on some work.**

Above left: **Zalman's flower coolers not only look fantastic, but they'll also cut out a lot of noise.**

078 > 079

Silence of the fans 2

> You can get enclosures for cutting out hard drive fan noise, but these don't provide any airflow over the drive, which can be dangerous.

Depending on your priorities, another way to make your PC cooler is to simply use slower components that don't require as much cooling. For example, some of the C3 processors integrated into VIA's EPIA motherboards (available from www.mini-itx.com) don't need a cooling fan at all, and even come with integrated graphics. If you just want a second, quiet PC to work on (you can forget playing games on this one), then these won't make any noise at all, particularly if you partner your PC with an external "power brick" PSU.

You can also reach a happy medium by getting a graphics card that's passively cooled. These aren't going to offer much in the way of 3D performance, but a passively cooled ATI All-In Wonder card (ATI's chipset with a 3D accelerator, TV tuner and video encoder/decoder in one) will be perfect for a PVR (personal video recorder), giving you all the features you need without sounding like a small helicopter.

A word of warning, though: it's never a good idea to get rid of all the fans in your PC. Unfortunately, it's in the nature of today's computer components to need some kind of airflow going over them to stop over-heating, even if they don't have a fan directly attached to them. Your motherboard chipset, for example, may only have a passive heatsink attached to it, which is fine with a bit of airflow, but it could overheat without it.

Another way to safely eliminate fans is by building your PC inside a ready-made heatpipe-based case that's set up to cool everything. A prime example is Zalman's TNN-500A, which has heatpipes (see glossary, p182) for cooling any CPU, GPU, and motherboard chipset, and even a fanless power supply system that's split up around the case. There isn't a fan in sight (or more importantly to be heard), and it's an ingenious piece of design with impeccable build-quality to match. There's just one problem with this solution—you have to pay for it. The TNN-500A isn't cheap. In fact, at the time this book went to press it cost around $1300—remember, that's just for the case and cooling system—so the noise of fans would have to really be annoying you if you felt you had to buy one.

There are also companies, such as Hush (www.hushtechnologies.net) and Tranquil (www.tranquilpc.co.uk), who make smaller heatpipe-based silent PCs that are much more affordable, and look good too, though their specs aren't quite as impressive.

It's worth noting, however, that fans don't create the only annoying noise in your PC, and once you've cut them out of the equation, you might soon notice the quirky chugging noises of your hard drive. You can get enclosures for cutting out this noise, such as the SilentDrive boxes available from www.quietpc.com, but these don't provide any airflow over your hard drive, which can be very dangerous with faster examples.

Thankfully, if you're prepared to put up with a small amount of fan noise, you can make your PC much quieter just by buying some alternative coolers for your parts. You can apply the alternative-fan theory to your CPU cooler as well as your case fans, and a quiet CPU cooler with a larger 92mm fan, such as Zalman's superb CNPS7000B "flower" cooler, will only cost around $40 and will cut down on a lot of the noise.

If you're feeling brave, it's also worth looking at an alternative cooler for your graphics card. The fantastic Arctic Cooling series of coolers cost just over $20 each, and they're much quieter than the standard coolers you get on graphics cards (there's a specific model for each graphics chip). The only problems with these are firstly, that they take up the space of two slots rather than the usual one, and secondly, you'll have to fit it yourself. This isn't as hard as it sounds, though, and if you take the time, keep your hands steady around the capacitors and follow the instructions, you'll have a quieter but equally powerful graphics card.

One fan that you won't want to mess with, though, is the one on your power supply. You can get water-cooled PSUs, and you can even get ones with passive coolers, but in my experience they don't output the wattage they should, they get incredibly hot, and they also cost far more than they're worth. Instead, get a decent power supply with a decent 120mm fan and you'll be able to build a cool, quiet, and powerful PC.

Above: **Some of VIA's EPIA motherboards don't require any active cooling, although they're about as fast as a depressed tortoise.**

Top left: **The SilentDrive hard drive case keeps drives quiet, but can overheat faster drives.**
Top right: **If you have space next to your graphics card slot, you can replace its whiny cooling fan with an Arctic Cooling silencer, which will quiet down that annoying graphics card fan.**

Above: **Hush's range of heatpipe-cooled PCs will look great under the TV, and they make absolutely no noise either.**
Right: **With a split PSU and heatpipes attached to everything, Zalman's TNN500A is the ultimate silent PC, although you could buy a small car for the same amount of money.**

Lighting

> Try using a UV light to expose your PC's innards, and then coat the parts that you want to glow with UV-reactive paint.

Lights are one of the easiest things to add to your PC, which is probably why they're so over-used by enthusiasts. Get carried away, and your PC will look more like the inside of a seedy New Jersey strip club than a cutting-edge masterpiece.

That said, a light or two can make all the difference to a mod project, especially in the dark, and they can also highlight your handiwork. The most common type of PC light is the cold cathode, which comes in a number of colors including red, green and neon blue. The most common sizes are 12in and 4in (although you can get models in all sorts of sizes if you look around), and they usually simply connect to one of your PSU's Molex connectors, with a switch to turn them on and off. Some sets come with a controller module, enabling you to control two lights from the same connector. This can be handy if you want to save your power connectors for more important things.

Before you buy enough lights to illuminate New York City, it's worth having a good think about what you want to light up in your PC, and where you'll need to position your lights. Ideally, you don't actually want to see the light units themselves, just the glow that emanates from them. One good place to mount a light is next to a large set of ventilation holes, which creates the effect of an eerie glow coming from your PC. If you've got a window in your case's side panel, then a single cold cathode light right next to the window's edge (but out of sight from the window) will show up your handiwork nicely.

Alternatively, try using a UV light to expose your PC's innards, and then coat the parts of your PC that you want to glow with UV-reactive paint. Take your time and special care when applying the paint, and this will look fantastic. If you've ever painted models or miniatures you'll know that one of the important tricks to learn is highlighting, where you use a lighter shade of paint to show up the bits that the light will hit first. This is the same technique you want to apply with your UV paint—just get a blob of paint on your brush, and then wipe nearly all of it off with a piece of kitchen towel. After that, use a dry brush to pick out the edges of your heatsinks' fins and you'll be able to see all their distinctive contours when the light is switched on.

A UV light can also be a great way to illuminate your water-cooling system. Add some UV-reactive additive to the water, such as Alphacool Powerfluid, and your tubing will light up like the insides of an alien spaceship when you flick the switch.

There are plenty of other forms of light that you can put in your PC. Try variants on the cold cathode strip, such as lights filled with bubbles, or just some neon string, which will light up whatever you wrap it around. The latter is great for marking out the outlines of parts, or even making a particular pattern behind a window mod. I also like the Knightlight kit (so called because it looks a bit like the front of KITT from *Knight Rider*), which has a series of lights going across a 5.25in drive bay panel, lighting up in a chaser sequence. Your supplier should be able to provide a 5.25in bezel to help you fit it into your drive bay.

Left: **Use a cold cathode to create an eerie glow behind a window mod.**
Far left: **Cold cathode lamps are the standard PC light, and they come in all sorts of colors, which makes it very tempting to fill your PC with a tribute to Vegas. Don't do this, however tempting it is.**

Opposite page, top right: **The ultra-cheesy bubble light is a popular variant of the cold cathode strip light.**
Main image: **Use neon string to highlight particular areas of your PC, or to fill gaps.**
Below left: **All you need is a Turbo Boost to take your PC right back to the '80s.**

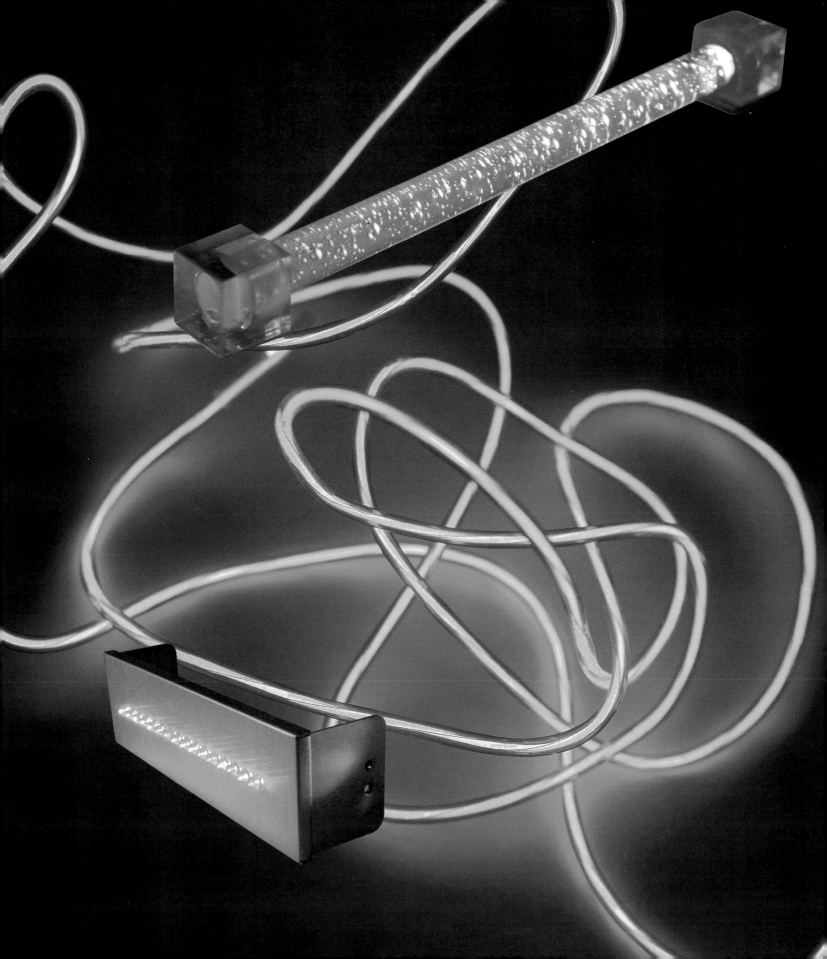

082 > 083

Cool stuff

> You can pick up an LCD screen from Radio Shack, wire it up to an internal COM port header and then program it yourself, but this isn't for the faint hearted.

Some people can never have enough flashing lights, and there's no need to stop at cold cathodes if you want your PC to look like it was delivered by a flying saucer. There are plenty of other cool bits and pieces that can be picked up cheaply, all can add an extra bit of pizzazz to your PC.

Ever since the digital watch came about in the 1970s, people have been drawn to LCD displays, and even now they can still impress your mates if you put one on the front of your PC. The best thing about displays for your PC, though, is that you can program them to say whatever you want, and react to certain programs. Which one you buy depends on how hard you want to make life for yourself. You can pick up an LCD screen from Radio Shack, wire it up to an internal COM port header and then program it yourself, but this isn't for the faint hearted.

The easiest way to add an LCD or VFD (vacuum fluorescent display—the light-up ones that you get in CD players) is to buy one that's built specifically to be put into a PC. A prime example is Matrix Orbital's range of USB screens (www.matrixorbital.com). These come with an application that enables you to program the display exactly as you wish. This includes your own choice of greeting when you turn on the PC (before it loads up Windows), as well as displaying graphic equalizer bars when playing music in Winamp and providing system information. The software is easy to use and is a great way to customize your PC with a

personal touch. You can also play on the fact that most of your mates won't know how easy it is to program and will assume that you have amazing programming and electronics skills.

The Matrix Orbital displays simply take up a 5.25in drive bay, and there are plenty of other drive bay fillers that can help you spruce up your PC. The most commonly found additions are system monitors, which can perform all types of functions, from adjusting the speed of your fans to telling you the temperature of your components, which can be very useful for measuring the environment of your overclocked components (see page 110).

However, getting a balance between looks and features is a difficult game of priorities with system monitors. For example, opinion is divided on Cooler Master's Musketeer, which has obviously been designed with looks as a priority over features—it can only control a single fan. However, if you don't need all the extra features and want something that looks great, then it's certainly worth a try. After all, a lot of customization is about showmanship, and this is no bad thing.

A fine example of the latter is top U.K. modder Mashie's new Spectrum analyzer (www.mashie.org/mdva), which produces a choice of eight light patterns over hundreds of red LEDs. Mashie originally designed this for his own anemone mod, but so many people liked it that he decided to have it produced, and you can now buy one for your own PC from www.kustompcs.co.uk.

Left: **Mashie's MDVA Spectrum analyzer.**

Above: **See your name in lights and pretend you've got awesome programming skills with a Matrix Orbital USB display.**

Below: **Cooler Master's Musketeer looks like a cross between a valve amplifier and a dashboard—and very pretty it is, too—but it won't tell you very much.**

084 > 085

Case mods

> Many modding shops offer transfers that look just like etchings and can be stuck onto a case window, saving time and money.

Of course, anyone can fill a couple of drive bays with system monitors and throw a couple of lights in their PC, but if you want your PC to look unique then you need to actually mod the case itself.

The most common case mod is the side panel window, designed to show off your system building skills as well as all your lights and expensive components. There are several ways to do this. The traditional one is to cut out a hole in your side panel using a jigsaw, being sure to mark up your cuts with a set square first, file it down to remove any sharp edges, and then fit a window into it. One way to do this is to buy a window kit from a modding shop, which will usually include a window of a particular size and some rubber to wedge it into place. Getting the window into the tight fit between the rubber and the hole can often be a cuss-inducing experience, but have patience, and you will get it done...eventually. If patience isn't among your many virtues, a far simpler way is just to drill four bolt holes around each corner of the hole, and then bolt your side panel in position.

However, as cases with windows now seem to be more popular than ones without, many case companies are offering cases with windows as standard, or a variety of "premodded" alternative side panels with windows. Sometimes the best way to get that professional finish is to cheat—it might not be as satisfying, but in many cases it'll look better.

Of course, as window mods are now mainstream, they aren't really going to make your case stand out that much anymore. This is why many modders customize their window a step further with an etching. You can do this yourself with careful use of a Dremel, or you can get an etching laser-cut by a professional. Both HotModz (www.xport1.com) and ThePCModShop (www.thepcmodshop.com) offer a laser etching service, which can cost from as little as $22.95 for one of their designs, or they can quote you a price on a design of your own. When designing your etching, bear

in mind that it needs to be simple enough to work in monochrome, and also the right shape and size to show off the insides of your PC. It can be a difficult balance to achieve. Of course, as with all these things, you can also cheat, and many modding shops offer transfers that look just like etchings, saving you a lot of money and time, even if you have no control over the design.

Another great way to customize your PC's look is to spray it with your own choice of color. This can be a long process if you want to do it properly, though. Simply buying a can of paint and spraying it on is not enough. To do the job well, you need to start by sanding off any existing paint, if there is any, and then priming the case. The rest of the process will involve gradually spray painting the case and sanding it down in between coats to ensure a blob and orange peel-effect free finish. You can, however, get specific sandpaper kits with the right grit-gradings for the job to make it easier. It can take well over a week to get this done, particularly if you leave the correct drying time in between sanding sessions, but the end effect should be fantastic.

Alternatively, if you have the money, try taking your PC case down to your local repair shop (make sure it's empty first) and asking how much it'll cost to give it a professional coat of paint. They might tell you to do something very rude—or more likely try to charge you a small fortune for the work—but you may just be able to strike a good deal, in which case, that professional paint job will be worth the expense.

If you don't have the skills (or the time and money) to spray paint your case properly, then another alternative is a CaseWrap (www.casewraps.com), a set of sticky-backed decals and panels that give your system that airbrushed look. Be warned: they can look fake or stupid, and you need to be careful not to get any creases in the panels during application. You're also stuck with a pre-made set of designs too, but if these are to your taste then there's nothing to stop you taking your PC customization down that road.

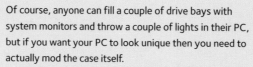

Left: **It'll take a lot of time and work to spray paint your case properly. If you've got the money, you could just take it down to the local car repair shop instead.**
Opposite, top: **Case wraps aren't to everybody's taste, but they offer another way to customize your system.**
Opposite, bottom left: **Shops such as KustomPCs sell** transfers that look just like etchings, although you have no control over the design.
Opposite, bottom right: **A professionally-applied coat of paint can make a massive difference to the look of a PC.**
Opposite, centre: **Some cases, such as this BeanTech Platinum, come with a range of different windowed side panels.**

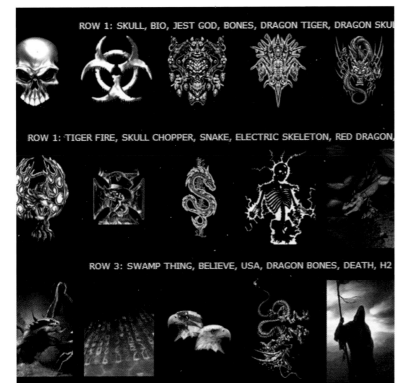

ROW 1: SKULL, BIO, JEST GOD, BONES, DRAGON TIGER, DRAGON SKULL

ROW 1: TIGER FIRE, SKULL CHOPPER, SNAKE, ELECTRIC SKELETON, RED DRAGON,

ROW 3: SWAMP THING, BELIEVE, USA, DRAGON BONES, DEATH, H2

086 > 087

Modding tools

> Cutting holes in a metal or plastic case will send sharp debris flying into the air. Make sure you wear protective glasses to stop it getting in your eyes.

So what tools do you need to start modding your case? There are plenty of options, but only are a few that are considered essential.

Let's start with the Dremel. You sand; Dremel sands. You cut; Dremel cuts. You wash the dog; Dremel washes the dog. You get the picture. The Dremel is the tool that you'll find modders mentioning the most frequently. In fact, the default caption for a newbie's avatar on www.bit-tech.net is "What's a Dremel?" The Dremel is what's known as a rotary tool, which is basically a drill to which you can attach other parts. These parts include cutting discs, sanders, polishers, and, of course, drill bits, just to mention a few.

The most common part you'll find modders using is the cutting disc, which can cut through just about everything—you just use a low speed for plastic (so it won't melt), and a higher speed for metal (so that it cuts, and also so that you can watch the cool sparks coming off it). Bear in mind, though, that the standard Dremel cutting discs are prone to breaking, and unless you want to replace 50 of them during a project, it's best to get some stronger stainless steel cutting discs.

Just like "Hoover" and "Kleenex," it's also worth noting that "Dremel" is just a brand name, rather than the name of a tool itself, and you can accordingly get cheaper clone models. Some of these are good, and some of them are fairly poor. If you do decide to go for a clone model, then make sure you get one that can use the standard Dremel parts.

My own personal advice if you're short on cash is to spend $50 on the entry-level, two-speed branded Dremel. This offers two speeds (one for plastic and one for metal), has solid build quality, and you can always get more accessories later. Meanwhile, if you have plenty of cash, the higher specification models come with more accessories and variable speed controls.

If you need to do some serious case hacking, then a jigsaw will get the job done in no time, plus you'll get to feel a bit like your dad when you're using it. Jigsaws are ideal for steel cases, which are tougher to cut than soft aluminum cases. They're also good for cutting wood—just make sure you get the appropriate saw blades for the material you're cutting and you'll be fine.

A Dremel and a jigsaw will let you cut your own custom designs, but sometimes you need much more accuracy than even the steadiest of human hands can offer. To cut a perfect circular hole for mounting a fan you can use another tool, named the holesaw. It's not a saw in the usual sense of the word, being a drill attachment, but the sharp blade (if that's the right word) on the end will cut a perfect hole in your case in no time. You will, however, need to get a holesaw that's up to the job, and (like jigsaws) there are blades for different materials. You'll need a hefty holesaw to cut out a 120mm hole in a steel case, and these cost around $20 for the blade alone. Your hardware store will always be able to tell you which saws are best for cutting which materials, so just ask if you're in any doubt.

Finally, you'll also need to finish off your cuts so that they don't have jagged edges and burrs hanging off them. Some sand paper can help out here, and I also recommend getting a set of needle files. These only cost a few dollars for a set of five, and they'll make it much easier to finish off your work smoothly.

One more warning; all of these cutting methods will send bits of sharp metal and plastic whizzing into the air. Make sure you wear protective glasses of some sort to stop all this getting into your eyes.

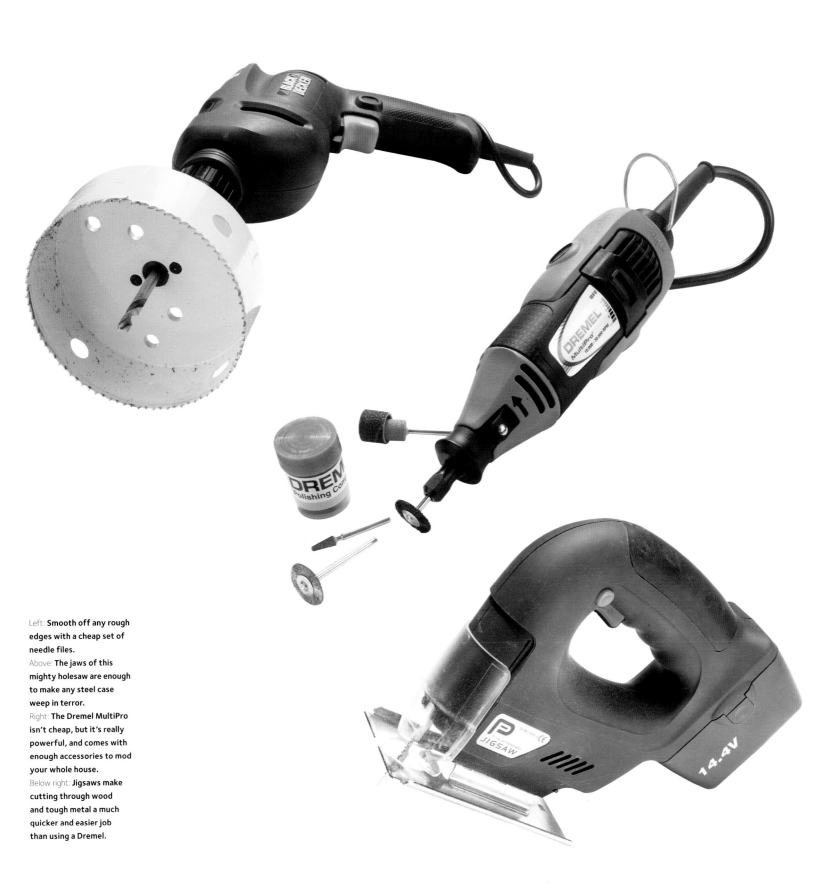

Left: **Smooth off any rough edges with a cheap set of needle files.**

Above: **The jaws of this mighty holesaw are enough to make any steel case weep in terror.**

Right: **The Dremel MultiPro isn't cheap, but it's really powerful, and comes with enough accessories to mod your whole house.**

Below right: **Jigsaws make cutting through wood and tough metal a much quicker and easier job than using a Dremel.**

Building and testing a system

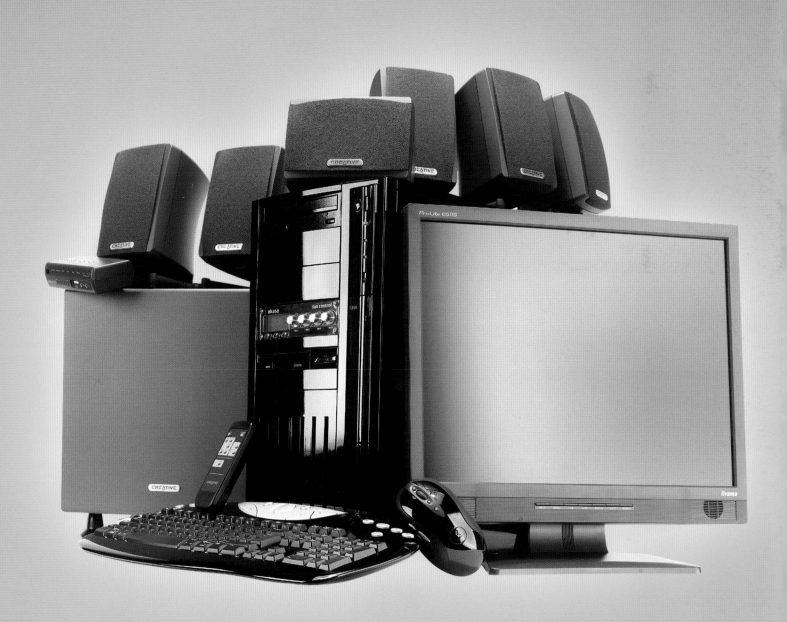

090 > 091

Building a system 1

> First of all, you'll need to ground yourself to prevent any static electricity damaging your components.

Years ago, I worked in a computer store, and it was common for customers to belittle our jobs by saying that PCs were just like a big jigsaw puzzle; you just needed to snap together all the pieces. Having decided not to pay a labor charge and build the PC themselves, they would invariably come back to the shop a few hours later, looking sheepish and with a box full of fried components. Building a PC wasn't as easy as they had thought. However, providing you learn the basic rules, there's nothing to stop you from doing it.

To start with, you'll need to ground yourself in some way to prevent any damaging static electricity being passed to your components. You can do this easily with an anti-static wristband, cheaply available from most electronics shops. The truth is that you can get by without one, but it's always better to be safe than sorry.

Now remove both side panels from your case and, if your case has a slide-out motherboard tray, slide this out before you screw in the motherboard—not having to lean over a case will make your life a whole lot easier. If your case doesn't have the slide out tray, you'll just have to fiddle around inside the case.

Before you start screwing your motherboard in, you'll need some standoffs installed between the motherboard and the tray. This is because the bottom of your board is covered with little bits of solder that hold all the connections in place, and if you connect all of these together with a big piece of metal underneath, you'll create thousands of instant short circuits and your board will go straight to silicon heaven. Your case should come with a bag of screws that also contains some standoffs—metal screws with a screw-thread in the top that you screw the motherboard into (you used to also get plastic standoffs, but these are much rarer now).

You need to screw these into the holes in your motherboard tray that correspond with the holes on your motherboard, so place the motherboard over the tray and note which holes will need standoffs, making sure that you've got a good spread that supports every corner of the board while holding it in properly.

Don't screw in the motherboard yet, as you can sometimes use the little bit of space underneath it to hide a few unsightly cables, particularly if they're flat IDE cables. If you have an IDE CD-ROM drive at the top of your case, then you can take the IDE cable underneath the motherboard, and then give it a neat 90° fold so that the connectors pop out right next to the IDE connector on the right of the motherboard. It's also worth thinking about where the rest of your cables are going to go while you're here too, particularly the ones snaking out from your power supply.

A big nest of power supply cables can make your PC look very messy, as well as prevent access for upgrading, so you want to make sure that you only have the cables you need going into the PC. You can then tie the rest away using cable ties. You need to think about this carefully before you start, so look carefully at which connectors you've got and where they'll be needed. It's also worth noting that some lines of cables from the PSU will have more than one Molex or PCI-E connector on them, and you will need to give each power-hungry component its own line, which means the other connectors can't be used. This doesn't affect your hard drive or optical drives, but it will affect your graphics card, as if it requires a separate supply, it's sure to drain a lot of power from it. Some graphics cards even require two connectors, and it's still worth making sure that both of these come from a separate line to ensure that each gets enough power.

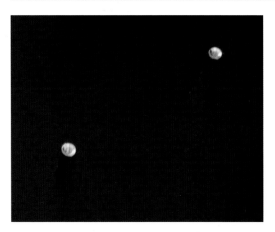

Far left: **Use standoffs and you won't fry your new motherboard when you screw it into your case.**
Left: **Use a power connector from a separate cable for each power-hungry component.**
Opposite, above: **You can use the clearance space under the motherboard to route flat cables out of the way.**
Opposite, below: **Line up your motherboard with your case and screw your standoffs into the appropriate holes.**

092 > 093

Building a system 2

> Always hold your components by the edges without touching the metal to avoid any static damage.

Once you know where all your power cables are going, keep them clear of the motherboard where possible—tie them up with some cable ties so that they don't trail everywhere. You can easily tie back the ones you don't need on the other side of the motherboard tray, and you can then (if you want to) put some spiral sleeving or braiding around the ones you are going to use to keep them neat and tidy. This can be quite a major job, especially as some sleeving will require you to remove the plastic connectors and put them back on afterwards, but some companies will braid your power supply for you for a fee, and some power supplies even come pre-braided.

Now that the major cables are routed efficiently, you can push the connector backplate that came with your motherboard into the appropriate space in your case, screw in the motherboard using the smaller screws that fit into the standoffs, and then start installing the components, which is actually a pretty easy job. Always remember to try and avoid any static damage; hold your components by the edges without touching the metal. Start with the memory. First, push back the white clips on either side of your DIMM socket, then line-up your memory module the right way round so that the notch in the middle is in the right place. Drop it into the slot and then, with a finger on each end, give it a hard push to click it into place. If the white clips click in then you've done it. Note that for dual channel memory configurations, your motherboard will require you to put your modules in specific slots. Refer to your manual to see which slots you'll need to use.

Now for the CPU. There will be a lever next to your CPU's socket, which you just need to pull out and then lift up. This will loosen the holes in the socket ready to take pins (or, if you're using an Intel LGA775 socket it will loosen the lid so that you can lift it up to insert your processor). You can now drop the processor in, lining up the big triangle (known as pin 1) with the big triangle on your socket. Carefully push the lever down to secure it in place (closing the lid first on an LGA775 socket). After that, spread some TIM onto the processor (see page 64) and put your heatsink into the standard clamp provided. Some heatsinks and waterblocks don't fit with these, so you may need to remove the plastic clamp from around the socket before you're able to fit these.

You can now install your graphics card. Your AGP or PCI-E slot will usually have a little notch or slider to pull out during installation, which you can then slot back in to hold the card in place. Look out for this before you insert the card. After that, you can then install your other cards, such as modems and sound cards, making sure that you leave at least one slot between them (and the graphics card) to ensure that there is enough airflow. All of your cards will screw in with the larger screws in your screw bag.

Finally, you need to install your drives. The hard drive cage inside your case should be removable, so take it out and screw in your hard drive with two screws on each side before putting the cage back in. Again, try to space your drives evenly if you have more than one, and position them as near to the front intake fan as possible to keep them cool. You will also need to do this with your CD-ROM drive or drives. If you can't remove the drive cages, then you may have to fiddle around on the other side to screw them in, but make sure they have two screws on each side or they may vibrate when they're running at full speed. This is not only potentially damaging, it also makes an extremely annoying noise.

Left: **Use some spiral wrap to bunch your cables together and keep them tidy.**
Far left: **Cable ties can stop stray wires obstructing access to your PC during future upgrades.**

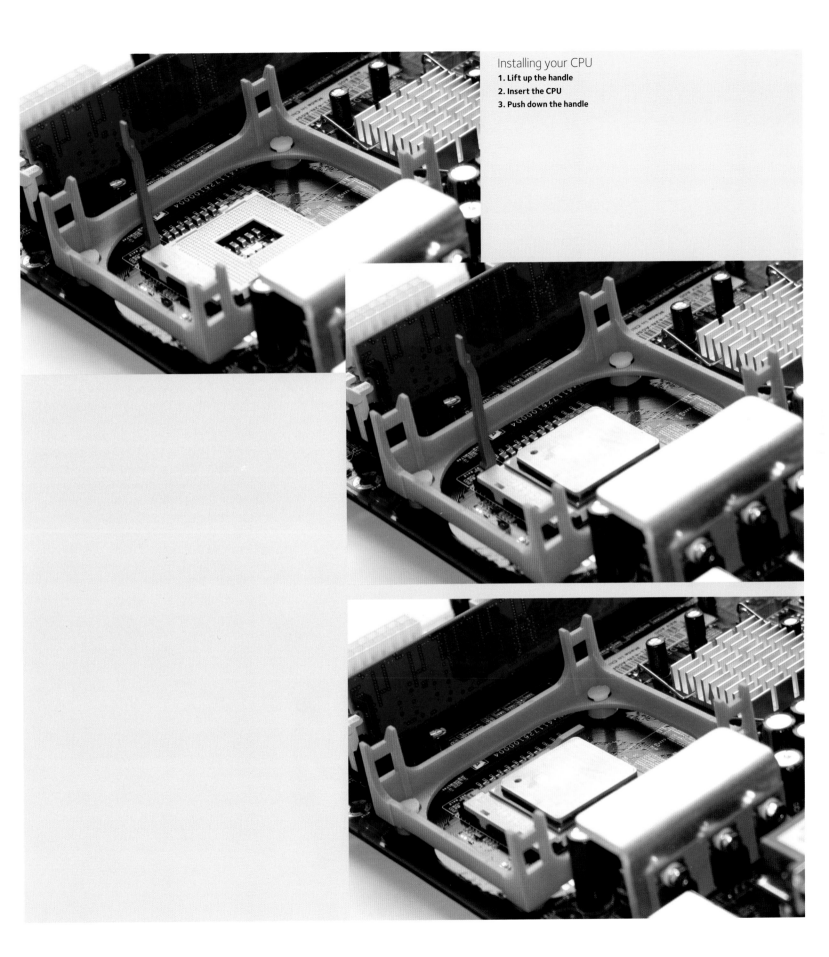

Installing your CPU
1. Lift up the handle
2. Insert the CPU
3. Push down the handle

Building a system 3

> The BIOS is where you can change your computer's settings at the lowest level, and it's also where you go to overclock your PC.

When all of that's done, you can then connect all of the cables to the motherboard and the components. These usually fit only one way around, but not always—some IDE cables will go in either way around so, as a general rule, you want the side of the cable with the red line to be closest to the drive's power connector. Also, if you're using an IDE hard drive rather than a SATA drive, ensure the jumpers on the back of the drive are set to "Master" (there will be a diagram on the drive showing you how to do this) and connect it to the Primary IDE slot. Then, for the best performance, you will need to do the same with your CD-ROM drive and connect it to the Secondary IDE slot. If you want to run more than one optical drive, then just set the second drive's jumper to "Slave" and hook it up to the second plug on your IDE cable.

Finally, you'll need to connect the power switch and the LED connectors to the correct pins on your motherboard, details of which will be included in the motherboard's manual. They may not work the first time, in which case just turning the connector around usually sorts it out. Having hooked everything up, connect your monitor to your graphics card, make sure the switch on your PSU is set to off (0), plug it into your wall socket, turn the power supply on (1), hit the power button on your computer and you should see your BIOS screen on your monitor.

When the display appears, it will say "hit <del> to enter Setup". Do this and you will be able to access your computer's BIOS (basic input output system). This is where you can change your computer's settings at their lowest level, and it's also where you go if you want to overclock your PC.

For the moment, though, you just want to make sure your PC is tuned to your needs. Start by going into the Standard CMOS Features section and make sure that the BIOS has picked up all your IDE drives correctly. If you have a SATA hard drive, then this may not be displayed in the BIOS, as these are usually detected by the separate SATA controller later on in the boot procedure. While you're here, you can also set the 1.44MB floppy drive to "None," unless you have a floppy drive.

You can clear out the rest of the bits you don't need in the BIOS by heading to the Integrated Peripherals section (also called Onboard Devices Configuration). Here you'll find all of your motherboard's ports and some of its features. Disable those you are not going to use to stop them taking up resources in Windows. If you have a USB printer, you can safely disable the parallel port; if you don't have any FireWire devices then you can disable FireWire and if you already have a sound card then you can disable your motherboard's onboard sound, if it has any.

After that, head to the frequency setting section and make sure that your memory timings are set to "By SPD." This automatically detects your memory's latency timings, and sets the BIOS accordingly. You can play about with these later, but at the moment you just want to make sure you have a stable system on which to install Windows.

Finally, you need to find the boot sequence section of the BIOS in the Advanced BIOS Features or Boot section of the BIOS, which basically determines which drives your computer will attempt to boot from first, second, and so on. To install Windows, you need to set the first boot device to CD-ROM. You can then insert your Windows CD, save the changes and exit, and your PC will automatically restart and begin the Windows installation.

Far left: **Connect your case's power switch and LEDs to the correct header—if they don't work, then just turn them the other way round and try again.**

Left: **If you're running two IDE devices off the same cable, then one needs to be set to Master, and the other to Slave.**

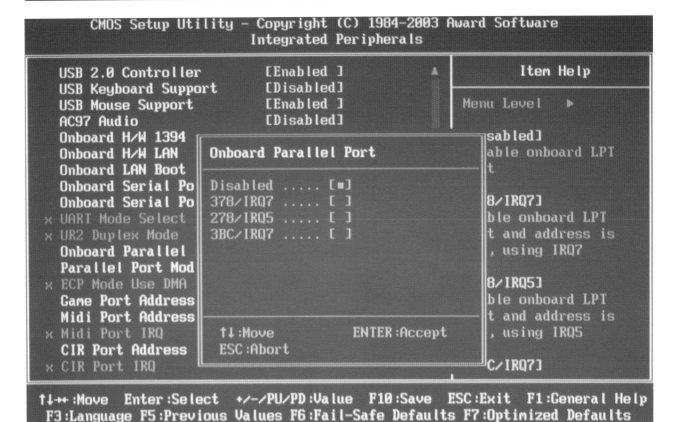

Above: **Set your first boot device to CD-ROM so that you can boot straight from the Windows installation CD.** Below: **Disable any prehistoric ports that you're not going to use. Otherwise, that parallel port will just use up valuable resources.**

096 > 097

Installing
Windows XP

> Don't use the drivers that come with the components, as these will be long out of date—download up-to-date drivers from the Internet.

So you've chosen the best components you could afford, fitted them into your case, painstakingly routed your cables, switched your machine on, and found it works (well, hopefully!). Your next job is to get Windows up and running. You might think this is as easy as throwing in a CD and letting Microsoft do all the work, but even installing Windows is an art form unto itself.

For a hassle free install you need a few things before you start: your Windows CD, a CD containing the latest Windows XP Service Pack (this is often available with magazine cover discs), and the latest drivers for all of your hardware. If possible, don't use the drivers that come on the CDs provided with your components, as these will be long out of date. Instead, download the most recent drivers using another computer with Internet access from the manufacturer's websites and burn them onto a CD before you begin.

Assuming you've set the first boot device in your BIOS to CD-ROM and you have your Windows XP CD in the drive, you just have to power up the PC to begin the installation. Once your computer has checked the memory and detected all your drives, it will go on to check your CD-ROM drive for a bootable CD and say "Press any key to boot from CD...." Agree, and the Windows installation procedure will begin.

A blue screen will come up, and one of the first things you'll see is the message "Hit F6 to install a third party RAID or SCSI controller." If you have an IDE hard drive then you don't need to worry about this, but if you have a SATA drive (or an IDE RAID array) then you need to hit F6 now and dig out the SATA driver disk from your motherboard box (or SATA controller box). Windows won't be able to find your hard drive without this.

After this, the Windows setup procedure will continue (as you don't want to repair an existing installation just hit Esc when it asks you to), eventually coming up with a license agreement for you to acknowledge. Obviously, you need to agree to this, so whether you're a Microsoft bashing anarchist or not, hit F8 and its time to set up your hard drive.

This procedure is called partitioning, which allows you to either setup your hard drive as one big block, or break it into several different virtual drives. Your best bet here is to set up a 10GB drive just to run Windows, and then use the rest of your space for installing programs and storing documents. This is firstly because Windows likes to have a lot of free hard drive space to use as virtual memory, and a dedicated 10GB partition will ensure that it has more than enough, and secondly it means you don't have to go through the pain of backing up all your gigabytes of data if you ever have to reinstall Windows.

To create a partition, press "C" when the menu comes up, and set the size of the partition to "10240." After that, press Enter to install Windows on that partition, and select NTFS for the format. The setup procedure will now install Windows on your 10GB dedicated partition.

Now it's just a question of letting Windows install itself, typing in your product key and entering the time and date at the appropriate points. About half an hour later you will be presented with the desktop. For some reason, Microsoft chose not to put My Documents or My Computer on the desktop at this point, so your first job is to put them there. To do this, right click anywhere on the desktop, select Properties, click the Desktop tab and then press the Customize Desktop button. From here, you just need to check the boxes next to My Computer and My Documents, hit OK and they'll appear on the desktop.

Right: **Set up a 10GB boot drive for Windows, and then partition the rest of your hard drive for programs and document storage.**

```
Windows XP Professional Setup

You asked Setup to create a new partition on
38147 MB Disk 0 at Id 0 on bus 0 on atapi [MBR].


    •   To create the new partition, enter a size below and
        press ENTER.

    •   To go back to the previous screen without creating
        the partition, press ESC.


The minimum size for the new partition is      8 megabytes (MB).
The maximum size for the new partition is 38139 megabytes (MB).
Create partition of size (in MB):  10240
```

Right: **Enable My Documents
and My Computer from the
Desktop Items menu.**
Below: **Your PC will soon
be able to run Windows in
its full glory, but there are
several other steps you
need to complete first.**

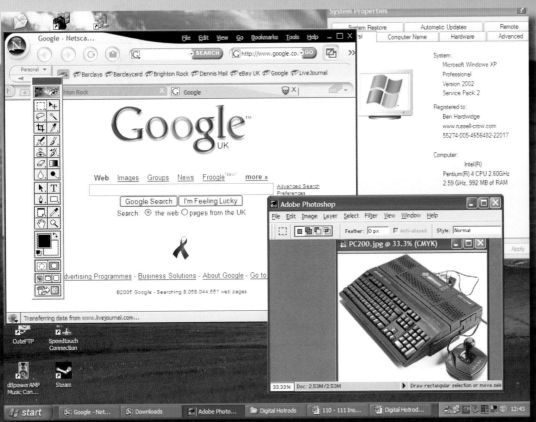

098 › 099

Installing
Windows XP 2

> Once all your drivers are
installed, the next job is
to install some anti-virus
and firewall software.

It's not over yet, though. Your next job is to make sure your version of Windows is up to date, so install Service Pack 2. Finished? Now it's time to install your drivers, making absolutely sure that you start with the driver for your motherboard chipset. Your motherboard is the foundation of your computer, so these drivers need to be installed first to ensure everything else installs correctly. Don't, whatever you do, install any other drivers before the motherboard driver or your PC is likely to get very screwy.

Once that's out of the way, install your graphics card driver, followed by the drivers for anything else you might need—keep in mind your motherboard should come with a USB 2 driver, as Windows XP won't pick up a USB 2 controller by default (yet). Quite a lot of driver installation routines require you to reboot your computer, so take this opportunity to go back into your BIOS and change the first boot device to your hard drive. This will make your computer boot up slightly quicker.

Now that all your drivers are installed, your next job is to install some anti-virus and firewall software. There are many free options available, so download these using another computer (if you can access one) and put them on a CD or some kind of pocketdrive. My favorites are Zone Alarm (www.zonelabs.com) and Agnitum Outpost Pro (www.agnitum.com) for firewalls, and Grisoft's AVG anti-virus package (www.grisoft.com).

It's now safe to set up your Internet connection and let Windows automatically patch any security holes that have been exposed by virus programmers.

Now that Windows is secure, your next job is to sort out the rest of the space on your hard drive that isn't being used. You can set this up any way you choose. Some people like to have separate partitions for video and music, some like separate partitions for all software. You can organize all of this space by right clicking on My Computer and selecting Manage. This will bring up your Computer Management options. To create a partition, right click on the box labeled "unpartitioned space", select New Partition, then choose the Extended Partition option. Make it into a logical drive, assign a letter to it and then format it with NTFS.

With your drive partitioned the way you want it, you just need to tell Windows to use your new partitions by changing the location of the default folders. By default, Windows will try to save certain files in their appropriate locations, such as My Pictures, My Documents, and so on. To move these folders to your new partition, you simply have to right click on them from the Start menu, select Properties, and then change the target drive letter with a colon and a backslash (D:\ for example).

That's the basic Windows set up out of the way, but there are all sorts of tricks you can now perform to get Windows running exactly the way you want it to.

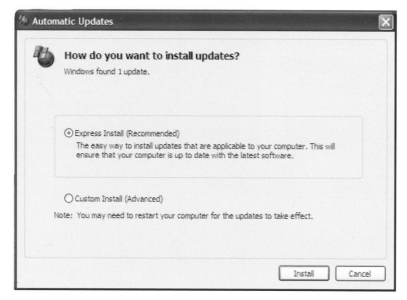

Left: **Let Automatic Updates patch any security holes in Windows for you.**

Right: **Use the Windows Disk Management tool to partition the rest of your hard drive as you want it.**
Below: **Install a firewall and an anti-virus package before you connect to the Internet. AVG and ZoneAlarm are available for free, so there's no excuse.**
Bottom right: **Move the My Documents folder to your chosen partition.**

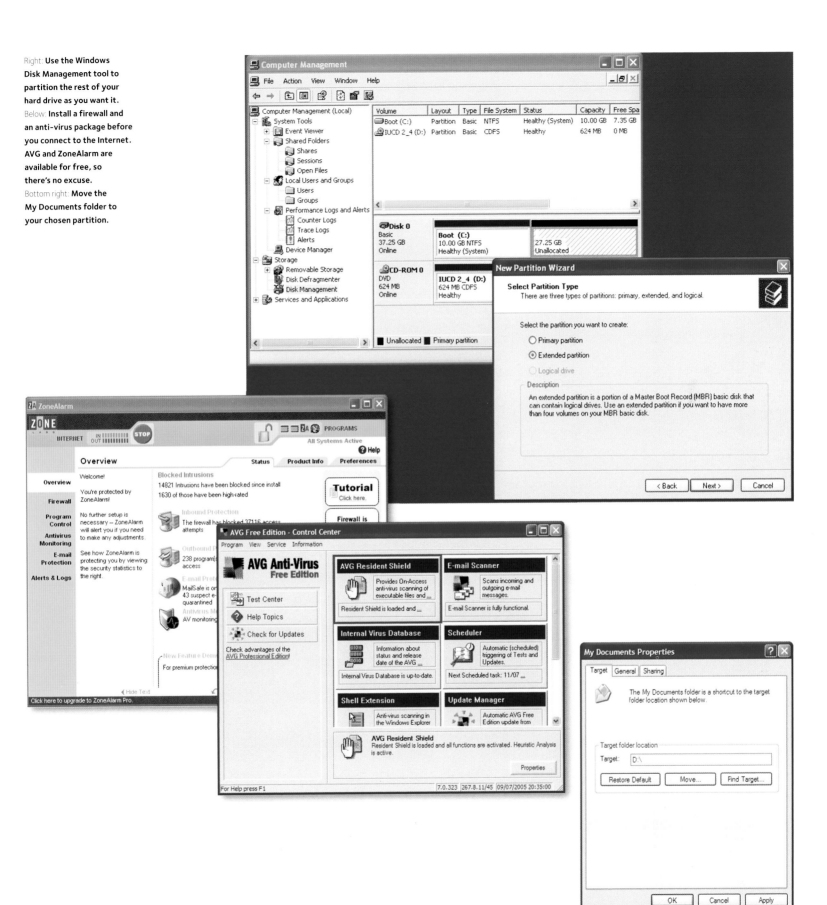

100 > 101

Optimizing Windows XP

> You can easily get rid of balloon tips and other minor annoyances by using a utility called TweakUI.

Of course, Windows will work fine as it is—there's nothing you need to do to it to make it function correctly, but then you could easily say the same thing about the PC you've just spent weeks building, tweaking, and overclocking. Do you really want a standard Windows install running on your custom PC? It makes about as much sense as spending $1,000 on a bottle of champagne, and serving it in plastic cups.

Start by speeding up your computer's hard drive access a using the Disk Defragmenter (under Accessories in the Programs menu). This will move all the scattered data on your hard drive into an orderly block, so that your hard drive's head doesn't have to move all over the place to retrieve data.

Now it's time to get Windows acting the way you want it to. Microsoft wants Windows to be usable for everybody, whether they're computer geeks or home economics teachers, and for this reason it has a few patronizing habits. One example is the balloon tips that pop up and point out the painfully obvious. You can easily get rid of these and many other annoyances with a handy little utility called TweakUI.

This tiny 147KB download can be grabbed from Microsoft's Web site at www.microsoft.com/windowsxp/downloads/powertoys/xppowertoys.mspx, and you can then run it by clicking on your Start button, selecting Run and then typing "tweakui" into the dialog box. A list of choices will then appear, and you just need to click on the various options to stop Windows doing those things you don't like.

Another useful friend that you can access from the Run box is msconfig—repeat the process used for starting TweakUI, typing "msconfig" instead. When this appears, you just need to click on the Startup tab and you can then uncheck any programs you don't want to run when Windows starts up. This can be very handy, especially for getting rid of those annoying obligatory programs that sometimes come bundled with free software downloads.

You can take this a step further by disabling any other services you don't need. Services are little processes that Windows runs in the background, some of which are essential, others that aren't. For example, if you know you don't need the Smart Card service, then you can disable it. The trick is to be very careful here, especially if you're not up to speed with what all the services do. Make sure you do a bit of research on the Web before you disable any essential services. Visit www.blackviper.com for more information concerning services.

You can disable services in msconfig (just hit the Services tab instead), but a far more user-friendly way of doing this is with a program called XPLite (a free trial version is available from www.litepc.com). This will again give you a set of checkboxes for all the things you can disable, with a brief description of what each one does. Not only that, it also gives you a full list of Windows components (anything from Solitaire to Disk Cleanup), which you can remove if you don't want them. You can do some of this from the Add/Remove programs section in the Windows Control Panel, but this list is much more comprehensive.

Below: **msconfig is a very useful tool that helps you cancel the services you don't need.**

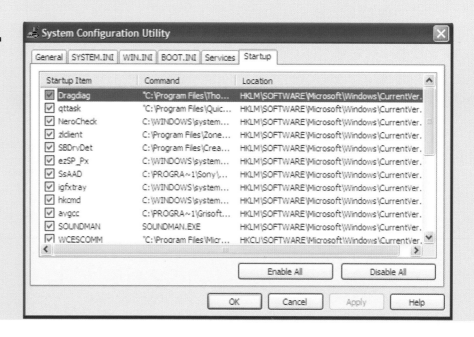

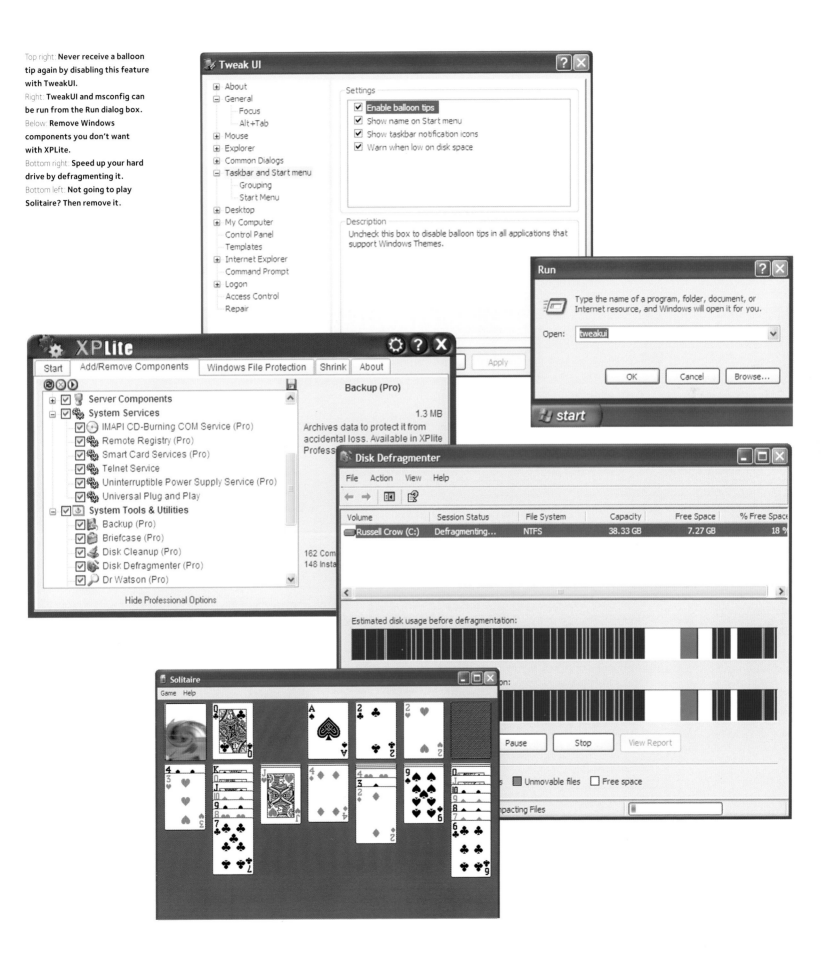

Top right: **Never receive a balloon tip again by disabling this feature with TweakUI.**

Right: **TweakUI and msconfig can be run from the Run dialog box.**

Below: **Remove Windows components you don't want with XPLite.**

Bottom right: **Speed up your hard drive by defragmenting it.**

Bottom left: **Not going to play Solitaire? Then remove it.**

Optimizing Windows XP 2

> A customized Windows install CD will allow you to include things like your motherboard's SATA driver, so you don't have to hit F6 at the beginning to install it.

One of the major keys to speeding up Windows is to have the latest drivers for your components. It's also crucial to get rid of the drivers already on your machine before you do this, especially if you're upgrading to a different component. You can usually remove these from the Add/Remove Programs part of your Windows Control Panel, but a far more efficient way is to use Driver Cleaner (www.driverheaven.net/cleaner). Driver Cleaner will not only uninstall your drivers, but also scan your computer's registry and system files for any leftover debris and make sure it removes every last trace. This not only saves on space, making your system boot up quicker, but it also ensures hassle-free driver installation.

When you're more familiar with Windows and it's time to build a new PC, you can actually make a customized Windows XP CD, as long as you have a CD burner, using a piece of software called nLite (www.nliteos.com). Again, this gives you a series of checkboxes for all the bits and pieces you may want, as well as the ability to put your motherboard's SATA driver onto the CD so you don't need to hit F6 at the beginning. This will give you a much more efficient Windows CD that you can use for installation next time around.

There are all sorts of other ways to tweak Windows, and you don't need to be a hardcore coder to perform them. Thankfully, several companies have produced programs that make the process much easier. A fine example is TweakXP (www.totalidea.com), which provides a convenient way to easily access various ways to alter Windows and its appearance.

A lot of this can be done directly through Window, but TweakXP makes everything much easier by providing instant access to those same choices. However, TweakXP, along with most Windows customization programs, will mess with your Windows registry, which can cause havoc with some software. It will probably be fine, but just in case, it's always worth setting up a System Restore point before you do anything. In fact, the program will prompt you to do so when you first start it up.

Once you're in, you'll find a whole range of goodies, including an option to create a RAM drive—useful if you have loads of memory—which can move your Internet cache to your RAM to speed up Web browsing. It will obviously clear it as soon as you shut down your PC.

Tweak XP doesn't stop at performance tweaks, though, and this is where Windows customization starts to get more exciting. After all, like modding, customization is as much about showmanship as it is about speed. The next step is to make Windows look exactly the way you want. TweakXP offers a good introduction to this, with options to change the size of your icons, as well as remove the Start button and Taskbar icons.

In fact, you can even remove the Windows Taskbar entirely—something which would be ideal for media PCs such as the DIGN (see page 142) where a big Windows Start button on the screen would spoil the overall effect.

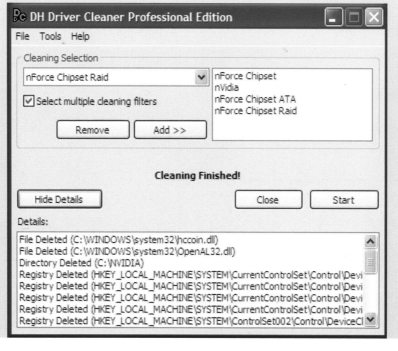

Left: **Driver Cleaner will get rid of any debris left in the registry from old drivers and ensure that your new drivers install smoothly. This is very handy when you're upgrading your graphics card from an NVIDIA card to an ATI card, or vice versa.**
Right, main image: **Shrink your icons down and remove the Taskbar and Start button completely with TweakXP.**

Opposite, top left: **Most Windows customization programs will alter your Windows registry, so create a System Restore point before running them.**
Opposite, top right: **Create a RAM drive for speedier data access.**
Opposite, inset: **Create a more efficient Windows XP CD for your next installation with nLite.**

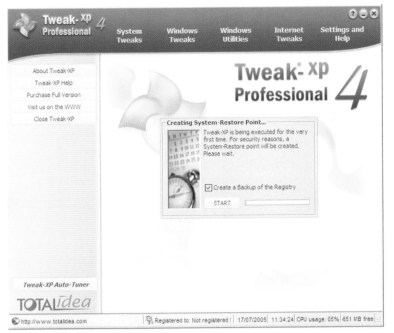

104 > 105

Customizing Windows XP

> It's in Windows' nature to be flexible, and you can change the way it looks and behaves with a few mouse clicks.

If you've ever had the misfortune to get into a conversation with a Mac enthusiast about computers, then you'll know that they just love to tell you how much better Macs are than PCs. Some of this is, of course, pretentious nonsense for the sake of being different, but there's also no getting around the fact that Mac OS X looks infinitely better than Windows XP.

It doesn't have to, though. It's in Windows' nature to be flexible, and there's no reason why you can't make Windows look exactly the way you want. This doesn't mean changing your desktop wallpaper and moving a few icons around; you can change the way Windows looks and behaves, and it can all be done with a few mouse clicks.

A great place to start is with a "skin;" a kind of façade on the front of a software package. You can skin many software packages, the most notable being the music player Winamp (www.winamp.com). However, you can also skin Windows, and this will change the look of just about everything you run in Windows, as well as the scroll bars and buttons.

There are various ways of doing this, but one of the easiest is to use a superb piece of software called WindowsBlinds (www.stardock.com), which comes with a range of pre-designed skins to customize the way Windows looks. Fancy a retro look? Then apply the surreal Windows 3.1 skin—even the Minimize, Maximize and Close buttons at the top of each application work in the same way that they did in Windows 3.1.

You can even emulate various generations of Mac OS, and once again the Minimize and Maximize traffic light buttons behave in the same way—with a cross appearing in the middle when you hover the mouse pointer over them. If you particularly like the Mac OS look, then it's also worth checking out ObjectDock (www.objectdock.com), which provides an easy-access rolling program dock, just like the one on Mac OS; the icons even grow as you move your mouse over them. If you combine this with the Taskbar-removal feature in TweakXP and a WindowsBlinds Mac skin, then you'll end up with a virtual Mac OS on your PC—the only difference being it will still run all those 3D games.

WindowsBlinds comes with a selection of skins to choose from, but these are constantly being added to, so it's always worth checking out other alternatives made by the community. Some of these are regularly added on the www.stardock.com website, but it's also worth looking at those available at http://skins.deviantart.com. Another good place to look for tips on skinning and customizing Windows XP is the "Customizing Windows XP" section of the forums at www.neowin.net.

Of course, the ultimate way to customize Windows is to design a skin yourself, and while this can be a lot of work, it'll certainly be rewarding if you have a good idea for a theme and have some artistic flair. You can do this with SkinStudio, again available from www.stardock.com.

Left: **Skinning Windows is as easy as clicking your mouse a few times.**

Opposite top: **Hey, it's just like Mac OS X. ObjectDock gives you a rolling program dock that's just like the one you'll find in Mac OS X.**

Opposite bottom left: **Ah, those were the days. Hankering for the Windows of days gone by? Run the retro Windows 3.1 skin.**

Opposite bottom right: **Windows Blinds offers a huge variety of skins for Windows XP, including this funky "Toon" skin.**

Mac OS X v 10.3

Internet Explorer

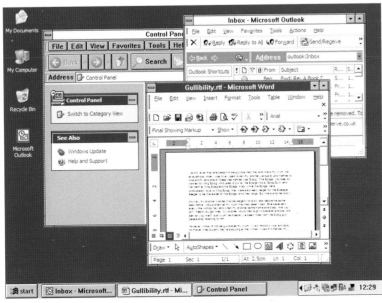

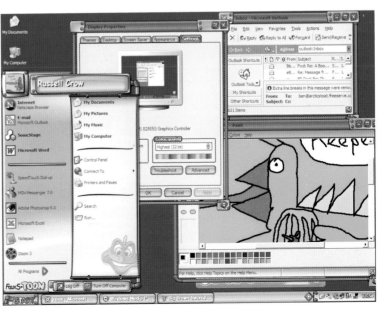

64-bit Windows XP and the future

> The main problem with Windows x64 edition is that at the moment it doesn't offer a lot over the standard 32-bit version.

Getting into the numbers game with computers is a dangerous business. It was easy to see that 16-bit computers and consoles were vastly superior to 8-bit systems, and the jump from 16- to 32-bit PCs was similarly awesome. Unfortunately, the same can't be said for 64-bit computing—at least not yet.

Initially, this might seem a bit mystifying. After all, being able to work with up to 64 binary digits surely provides infinitely more computing power? Well, yes, it does, but you need to remember that 32-bit computing has actually provided pretty much all we've needed for computing so far. It's going to take a long time for 64-bit computing to make the same kind of impact.

That said, the future prospects for 64-bit computing are really exciting. Game developers are talking about free-roaming worlds that measure miles across, requiring a vehicle to get from one place to another, as well as more realistic physics processing. Not only that, but 32-bit computers can't currently address more than 4GB, whereas a 64-bit computer will theoretically be able to access up to 18 billion gigabytes of memory. Obviously, we'll have to wait for memory to come down in price significantly before most computers push the 32-bit 4GB limit—let alone 18 billion gigabytes—but there's no question that the future of PCs will be 64-bit.

In fact, the 64-bit revolution has already started, with both AMD's AMD64 range of processors and Intel's latest EM64T Pentium D and Extreme Edition processors supporting both 32- and 64-bit software. Microsoft too has just released a new version of Windows XP, called Windows XP Professional x64 Edition, which is backwards-compatible with 32-bit software.

However, it is not compatible with 32-bit drivers, so before heading down this path, you will need to make sure you have 64-bit drivers for every piece of hardware you own, from the motherboard chipset to the expansion cards, as well as any Bluetooth or Wireless LAN USB thumb drives you have. It's also worth noting that (unlike 32-bit Windows XP) x64 Edition won't run any 16-bit software. This isn't a problem for the most part, but some older games from the Windows 98 era have reportedly had problems running on it.

The main problem for Windows x64 Edition, though, is that at the moment it doesn't offer a lot over the standard 32-bit version. A few programs, such as WinImage and VirtualDub, have 64-bit betas available, but the performance difference between 32-bit and 64-bit versions is minimal. Windows MovieMaker, bundled with the OS, has also been updated to a 64-bit version, but when I tested this it only knocked a few seconds off encoding times—hardly a quantum leap in technology.

A few game developers have released 64-bit patches for games, allowing them to take advantage of the new OS, but again the differences are minimal. A 64-bit patch for *Far Cry* is available from www.amd.com/farcry, but while it looks slightly different, it's fair to say that the changes wouldn't be out of the league of a decent 32-bit processor, and it's nothing like the visual jump to High Dynamic Range (HDR) imaging.

Interestingly, there's as yet no retail version of Windows XP x64 Edition; you have to buy an OEM version with a piece of Microsoft-certified hardware (such as a mouse). Basically, if you're building a 64-bit PC (which you should be by now), then you may as well buy Windows x64 Edition, but if you've already bought Windows XP, then there really isn't a lot of point in buying the new 64-bit OS, even if it does give you a new 64-bit Windows wallpaper and loading screen. 64-bit computing will take off, but it's not a necessity for now.

Opposite: **Windows XP x64 Edition might get you new wallpaper and a different loading screen, but it doesn't offer a whole let else at the moment. Although it will run 32-bit, as well as 64-bit software...**
Right: **...it won't run any 32-bit drivers, so make sure you have 64-bit drivers for all of your components.**
Opposite, top: **The special 64-bit edition of *Far Cry* looks slightly different, but it's not nearly as big a leap as the HDR version.**

32-bit

64-bit

108 > 109

Overclocking— an introduction to the dark art

> The risk in overclocking isn't as big as component manufacturers would have you believe, but it is still possible to fry your new chip.

Left: **Overclocking could allow you to run a 2.6GHz processor at over 3GHz, giving you loads of extra speed for free.**

You've probably already heard the term "overclocking," even if you don't actually know what it means. Sadly, the term has nothing to do with fitting too many appointments into an already busy schedule. Instead, it describes a fine art now practiced by many, from teenage geeks, to dodgy managers of computer shops.

In basic terms, overclocking can be defined as running a computer component faster than its intended speed, meaning you effectively get a faster part without having to pay for it. For example, purchasing a 2.6GHz Pentium 4 and overclocking it to 3GHz. This not only saves you a few dollars, it also gives you the satisfaction of knowing that you've got something that the masses do not.

It's debatable when people first started overclocking, but there are a few tales of people even overclocking 8086 processors in the early 1980s, as well as early home computers. These early Einsteins would have required some seriously in-depth knowledge of the hardware they were dealing with, so it's fair to say that overclocking has only recently become more widespread.

Overclocking became a mainstream buzzword when Intel updated its Slot 1 Celeron processors to contain 128KB of Level 2 cache (the previous Celerons had no cache at all). Not only that, but—unlike the flagship Pentium II chips—the new Celeron's cache was actually on the chip, rather than on the circuit board next to it, meaning that it could be accessed slightly quicker.

This in turn meant that all the informed PC enthusiast had to do was spend $100 or so on a 300MHz Celeron A chip, increase the front side bus (see glossary, page 182) speed of their motherboard from

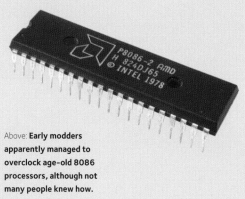

Above: **Early modders apparently managed to overclock age-old 8086 processors, although not many people knew how.**

66MHz to 100MHz, and they would effectively have a 450MHz processor with a 100MHz front side bus, which would be almost as fast as a $700 Pentium II/450.

Overclocking really started to take off when you could buy motherboards that allowed you to adjust the front side bus and the CPU's multiplier (see glossary, page 182), circa the original Pentium era. This made your options much more flexible; you could control the speed of your whole PC, not just the processor.

However, you had to adjust these settings using switches on the motherboard, meaning that you had to take your PC apart if you wanted to overclock it. Not until the end of 1999 did motherboards start to appear that allowed you to adjust the front side bus directly through your motherboard's BIOS (see glossary, page 182). Suddenly, overclocking was as easy as just pushing a couple of buttons.

So why is it a dark art? Well, firstly, there's the risk involved. This isn't as big as component manufacturers would have you believe, but overclocking can fry your shiny new chip as well as invalidate any warranty. There's also the fact that the likes of Intel really don't like it. In fact, Intel was quick to put a lock on the multipliers of its chips as far back as the original Pentium era in order to make them harder to overclock efficiently. It was only in 2004 that motherboard manufacturers managed to find a way around this lock.

Despite Intel's best efforts, overclocking is now huge, and there are utilities available to help you not only overclock your CPU, but also your memory and graphics card. Over the next few pages we'll introduce you to the basic principles you'll need to get started.

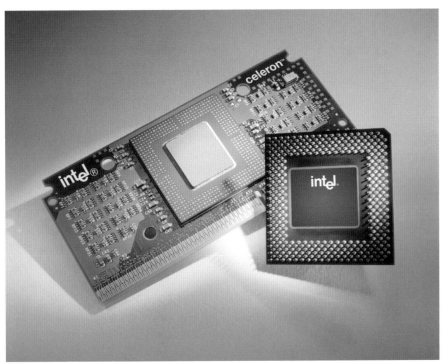

Left: **Many 300MHz Celerons could run at 450MHz, and when word got about, overclocking became much more mainstream.**

Above: **You used to have to overclock your PC by using switches on the motherboard, but you can now do it through your motherboard's BIOS.**

Below: **Refrigeration systems, such as Asetek's VapoChill, allow you to overclock your PC even further.**

Above: **It may have an integrated memory controller, but you can still overclock the Athlon 64's HyperTransport bus to get the same effect.**

Overclockable components

> Each silicon wafer will be packed full of CPU dies, and not all of them will be given the same speed grade even though they are essentially the same processor.

The first thing to bear in mind with overclocking is that some components are more overclockable than others. For a start, there are simple differences between processors. As we've already established, the Pentium 4 is generally more overclockable than the Athlon 64 because its lower transistor-count creates less heat. This is only a general rule, however, and some Athlon 64 chips, such as the 3000+, can be overclocked to the hilt. Unlike high-end Pentium chips, the Athlon 64 FX also has unlocked multipliers, making it ideal for overclocking.

Certain models of processor are generally more overclockable, and this is all down to the way that they are made. Processors are produced on wafers: large, circular discs of silicon. A wafer will be packed full of CPU dies, and you can guarantee that not every single one of them will be given the same speed grade, despite the fact that they're essentially the same processor. Each CPU die will be tested to see which speed grade it meets, so a 2.6GHz Pentium 4 could easily be a 3GHz Pentium 4 that didn't quite meet the mark.

However, there are occasions when Intel or AMD just need to push out huge numbers of processors with lower speed grades to meet higher demand. These processors, which will be marked with a speed grade far lower than their actual capability, are the ones you want for overclocking. With this in mind, it's worth keeping your eye on technical magazines and websites to see what the latest overclockable chips are. One recent example was the Athlon XP 2500+ M. It came off the same wafer as the Athlon XP 3200+, and thus gave you a lot of speed for a very cheap price. Some companies will also specifically purchase chips like this that can be overclocked.

This, though, is a game of chance. In some cases, the chips have been marked with a lower speed grade simply because they didn't meet the test requirements. Also, the overclocking ceiling of a component varies between every one manufactured. It's never a clear-cut case of "this processor can be overclocked by exactly this number of megahertz." You may well find that your

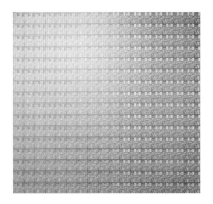

Above: **A Pentium 4 wafer—all those little squares are CPU dies, and not all of them will be given the same speed grade.**

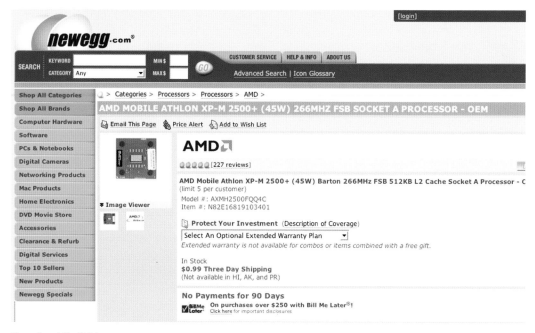

Above: **Search the Web to find sites selling processors popular with overclockers.**

processor's overclocking ceiling is greater than what's listed in magazines and on websites, but you may also find the opposite. It's a gamble, but one that's often worth taking. You are, after all, buying cheap components.

You will also find that your CPU's stepping (see "What is Stepping?", right) can have an effect on how far it can be overclocked. One 3.2GHz Pentium 4 isn't necessarily the same as another, as Intel constantly refines the manufacturing process of its chips. You can, however, get a fair idea if you can find out the particular stepping of your CPU. Each generation of a type of CPU will be given a particular stepping for each change, so check out the websites to see which kinds of stepping can offer the best overclocking potential.

Similarly, you will also find that some graphics cards, motherboards, and memory modules can be overclocked much higher than others. Some of this comes down to luck, but some of it also comes down to the quality of the components used. Gainward's "Golden Sample" graphics cards, for example, use the very best

chips that come off the NVIDIA production line and arrive pre-overclocked and guaranteed. Again, you can get a pretty fair idea about which components will run at the higher clock speeds by checking out reviews, but don't assume that your component will be exactly the same.

Generally, heat is the biggest hindrance to overclocking, so the components that have a smaller number of transistors are likely to overclock higher. With this in mind, it's worth looking at the manufacturing process of a component. The size of the spaces between transistors is measured in nanometers, and with smaller transistors you can afford to spread them out over a wider area and not create so much heat. This is why ATI's Radeon X800, which is fabricated on a 110nm production process, is generally much more overclockable than the Radeon X800 Pro, which is fabricated on a 130nm production process.

What is Stepping?

Like everything else in the computer industry, processors aren't usually perfect from the word go. As Intel or AMD finds odd bugs or discovers ways to improve manufacturing standards, they revise the processors. This "stepping" or "revision number" as AMD calls it, is a code that describes what particular revision the processor in question is. You can find the stepping of your processor using popular utilities such as CPU-Z (downloadable from www.cpuid.com). You can also find a chart of the stepping on Intel's CPUs at: http://processorfinder.intel.com/scripts/list.asp

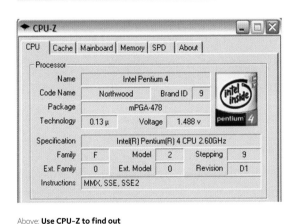

Above: **Use CPU-Z to find out your CPU's particular stepping.**
Right: **Gainward's "Golden Sample" range of cards come with the cream of NVIDIA's chips, and are pre-overclocked.**
Far right: **If you can find out the stepping of your CPU, then you're a step closer to knowing its manufacturing process.**

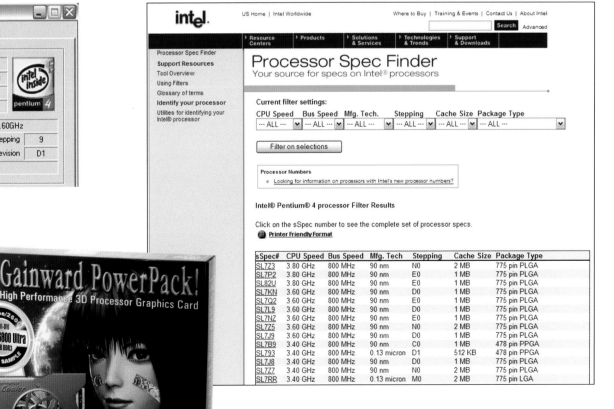

Intel® Pentium® 4 processor Filter Results

sSpec#	CPU Speed	Bus Speed	Mfg. Tech	Stepping	Cache Size	Package Type
SL7Z3	3.80 GHz	800 MHz	90 nm	N0	2 MB	775 pin PLGA
SL7P2	3.80 GHz	800 MHz	90 nm	E0	1 MB	775 pin PLGA
SL82U	3.80 GHz	800 MHz	90 nm	E0	1 MB	775 pin PLGA
SL7KN	3.60 GHz	800 MHz	90 nm	D0	1 MB	775 pin PLGA
SL7Q2	3.60 GHz	800 MHz	90 nm	E0	1 MB	775 pin PLGA
SL7L9	3.60 GHz	800 MHz	90 nm	D0	1 MB	775 pin PLGA
SL7NZ	3.60 GHz	800 MHz	90 nm	E0	1 MB	775 pin PLGA
SL7Z5	3.60 GHz	800 MHz	90 nm	N0	2 MB	775 pin PLGA
SL7J9	3.60 GHz	800 MHz	90 nm	D0	1 MB	775 pin PLGA
SL7B9	3.40 GHz	800 MHz	90 nm	C0	1 MB	478 pin PPGA
SL793	3.40 GHz	800 MHz	0.13 micron	D1	512 KB	478 pin PPGA
SL7J8	3.40 GHz	800 MHz	90 nm	D0	1 MB	775 pin PLGA
SL7Z7	3.40 GHz	800 MHz	90 nm	N0	2 MB	775 pin PLGA
SL7RR	3.40 GHz	800 MHz	0.13 micron	M0	2 MB	775 pin LGA

Overclocking the CPU

> You always want to overclock using the front side bus first rather than the multiplier, as this speeds up your whole PC.

Whether you genuinely need the extra performance, or perhaps just like the sound of a nice round 3GHz figure over a clunky 2.6GHz one, overclocking is an easy way to get more speed for free. What's more, overclocking your CPU is surprisingly easy, if time-consuming.

Start by entering your BIOS, and finding the section called "Frequency settings" or something along those lines. Your CPU's speed is generally determined by two factors. The first is the front side bus (FSB), which is the speed your whole motherboard (and most of the things plugged into it) runs at. The second factor is the multiplier, which multiplies the FSB speed by a specific amount to achieve the processor speed.

It's also worth noting that AMD's AMD64 chips don't use an FSB, as the memory controller is built into the CPU. Luckily, you can achieve the same effect by adjusting the HyperTransport bus. Also, don't be confused by the strange bus speed figures often quoted for the Pentium 4. The Pentium 4 has a quad-pumped bus that, like a CPU multiplier, multiplies the FSB by four to speed things up a bit. The figure you'll be adjusting in the BIOS, however, will somewhere around 200MHz (not 800MHz), and this is also the figure your CPU multiplier will be multiplying.

Another point to bear in mind is that while some of AMD's chips let you change the multiplier, Intel's chips have a multiplier lock to stop you doing this. For this reason, overclocking an Intel system generally involves increasing the FSB speed, while overclocking an AMD system often involves just increasing the CPU's

multiplier. However, at the time of going to press, both Asus and AOpen had produced BIOS upgrades for their motherboards that circumvented this, and we're expecting more motherboard manufacturers to follow suit. This is great news, because you want as much flexibility as possible.

Your first step is to find your maximum FSB (or HyperTransport) speed—so take this up in your BIOS, by a small amount (say 5MHz), save and exit your BIOS and then go into Windows. You'll now want to run a benchmark (see page 122–131), firstly to see if your computer's stable at the new settings, and secondly to see what difference the change has made to your PC's performance. It's best to use a benchmark that lasts a long time and stresses the system in ways you'll be using it—3DMark is quite adequate here, as it not only simulates games but also has a specific CPU section that stresses out the processor. If it completes the benchmark, then write down the benchmark score, reboot the PC and take the front side bus up by another 5MHz and repeat the whole process again.

Keep repeating this until your benchmark starts locking up or becomes unstable, and then go back down to the previous setting, drop the CPU multiplier by one level and go through the whole process again until you get the highest possible FSB and CPU speed. You always want to overclock using the FSB first, rather than just the multiplier, as this speeds up the whole PC rather than just your processor. You can, after all, only go as fast as your slowest component.

Above: **Pentium 4s have locked multipliers, but a BIOS upgrade can sometimes offer a workaround.**

Right: **Increase your front side bus speed by small increments.**

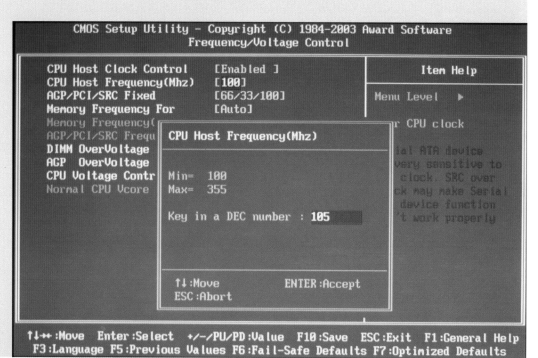

FPS: 7   Time: 0:02.78   Frame: 31

Above: **Use a stressful benchmark like 3DMark05 to check that your system's still stable.**

Left: **That's 220 extra 3D Marks and we didn't even change the processor!**

Right: **Why pay more for Intel's latest chip when you can get it for free?**

Overclocking the CPU 2

> Start by taking the CPU voltage up by around 0.025V. If the system is still stable, then try a similar increase but don't go much beyond this unless you've got some serious cooling.

The main problem that overclocking is likely to cause is instability in your system, the side effects of which could include your PC locking up or rebooting itself. This isn't necessarily because you're pushing your CPU beyond its clock speed. It may be that your CPU just needs more power to churn out all those extra megahertz.

Your CPU will be assigned a default voltage that supplies enough power to run at its default clock speed, and your motherboard's BIOS should pick this up automatically. Your BIOS should also let you change your CPU's voltage, and you can sometimes find that increasing the voltage a little can give your CPU the power it needs to cure your instability issues.

You need to be cautious when you're doing this, though, and start by taking the voltage up by just one notch (say 0.025V). If your system is still stable then try taking it up another notch or two, but don't go beyond this unless you've got some serious cooling for your CPU. Any form of overclocking will make your CPU much hotter than usual, and you'll need to compensate for this with an alternative heat sink and fan setup, or even a water-cooling system. However, increasing your CPU's voltage will create even more heat on top. Be careful—you don't want to end up toasting your CPU.

You'll find that most of the BIOS systems in today's motherboards will have a temperature probe for measuring the temperature of your CPU, and this can be very useful for gauging how efficient your cooler is, as well as seeing if your CPU's temperature is in the danger zone. Ideally you want your CPU's temperature to be under 104°F (40°C) and certainly no higher than 149°F (65°C), although you

can probably risk it being higher if you keep an eye on it. Every CPU will have a specified maximum operating temperature, which can be as high as 194°F (90°C), but it's best to keep it well under this. One important thing to note here, is that the temperature you'll see in the BIOS is when your CPU is idle, and its temperature will increase dramatically when it starts working hard with real software. Some motherboard manufacturers, such as Asus, provide a Windows utility to probe your motherboard's temperature, which means you can find the temperature when you're running real software. If your motherboard comes with anything like this, use it. Of course, if you've got a spare drive bay, you could also install a system monitor with a temperature probe, too.

Another thing to bear in mind when overclocking your CPU is that many of today's processors are aware of when they're being pushed beyond their capabilities, and will start to throttle back when pushed too hard. This is good because it stops your system crashing and protects your CPU, but it can also have the adverse effect of making your CPU slower than it was before you started overclocking it. There is, however, a great utility called ThrottleWatch (download from www.panopsys.com) that, via a graphic display, allows you to keep an eye on your CPU's performance. If you see your CPU throttling then reduce its speed to a more comfortable level.

Your best bet is to run something really intensive, such as the protein folding medical research program Folding@Home (available from http://folding.stanford.edu/download.html), which will push your CPU to its limit. If your machine's okay running this application, you should be good to go.

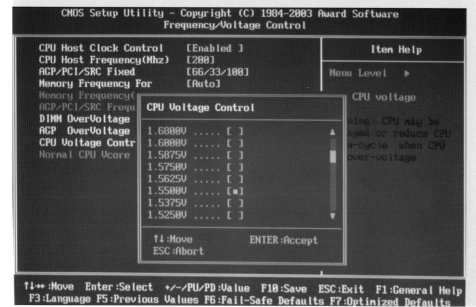

Left: **Increase your CPU's voltage by small increments.**

Below: If your CPU can run at 100 percent without throttling, then you have an efficient overclock.

Right: Run a CPU-punishing application like Folding@Home to push your processor to its limit and see if it throttles.

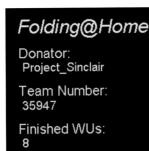

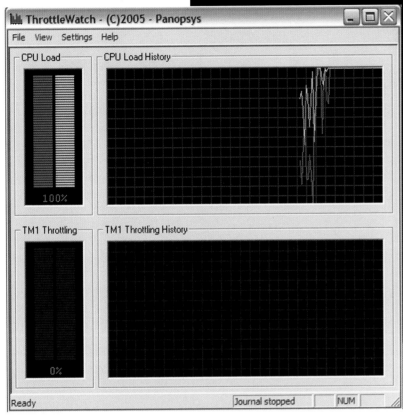

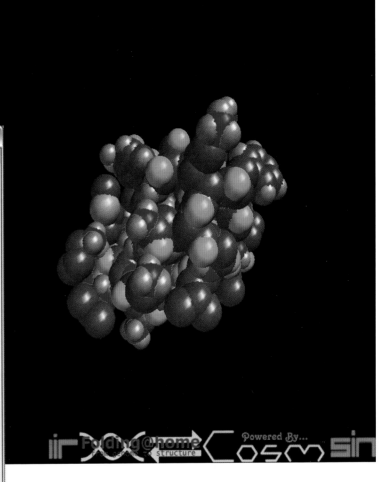

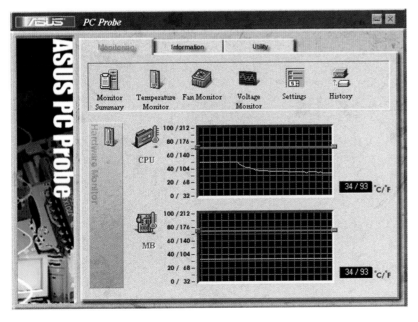

Left: If your motherboard came with a temperature monitoring utility, such as Asus' PC Probe, then you can use it to see how hot your CPU gets when it's running real software.

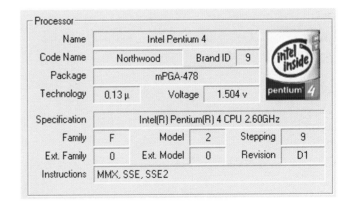

Above: A small increase in voltage can buy you some more overclocking headroom, but it will also generate more heat.

It's all about timing

> The CAS is the most important latency setting, as it's the one that will make the most difference to the speed of your system.

Any good comedian (and probably some pretty bad ones too) will tell you that a lot of your success is down to timing. The same goes for memory. Get this wrong and your machine could end up like an episode of "Saved by the Bell"—it'll just about work, but it won't be anything to be proud of. You can overclock memory in the same way that you can overclock any component, but there's another complication, which is latency.

Latency basically refers to the number of clock cycles your memory will take to complete a task, and this is split into four figures. The order in which these figures appear depends on the memory manufacturer or retailer. There's no hard and fast rule, but for the purpose of this book, I'm going to take them in order of tRAS, tRCD, tRP, and CAS. An example of this would be a timing of 12-4-4-4.

Let's start with the tRAS, which is the big fat number that's distinctively larger than the others. This is because the tRAS (also known as the RAS pulse width, or sometimes simply "cycle time") is the number of clock cycles that your memory will take to close after it's been activated, so that it can be written to again. As a general rule, the tRAS should be just a little bit higher than your CAS + tRCD + 2, although this varies between modules, and you can sometimes survive with less.

Next up, we have the tRCD (also known as RAS to CAS delay). As you may or may not know, memory addresses work in terms of rows and columns of numbers. For this reason, you have both RAS (row address strobe) and CAS (column address strobe). The tRCD is simply the number of clock cycles that your memory will take to get a column address from the CPU after it's received the row address.

The third setting is tRP (also known as RAS precharge), which is the time your memory will take to activate a row after a precharge command. A precharge command is basically an instruction to charge up its storage capacitors. In simple terms, your memory will get to work quicker if this is lower.

Finally, we have the CAS (column address strobe), which is the most important of the latency settings and the most commonly quoted. This is the setting that's most likely to make your system noticeably quicker or slower, as well as making it crash if it's set too low. The CAS is basically the number of clock cycles that your memory will take to start working on a read command after it's received all the other information.

Your memory will usually have its latency timings somewhere in the packaging or on the memory module itself. Your best bet is to start by setting your memory

Right: **Latency timings are usually provided on your memory modules or their packaging, although there's no rule as to what order they'll be in.**

timings to "By SPD" in the BIOS. This makes your computer self-detect the timings from the memory. After that, you can start to play around.

Bear in mind, though, that changing your memory's latency timings only makes a fractional difference to performance compared with most tweaks, so this is only for true performance connoisseurs. You're unlikely to see a performance difference in most standard benchmarks above the benchmark's usual margin of error. To measure any performance difference, run a synthetic memory bandwidth benchmark (there's one in SiSoft Sandra) and check which settings provide the biggest jump in performance while still remaining stable.

It's also worth noting that reducing your latency timings can also hinder your overclocking potential in a big way. If you have the memory set to "By SPD" in the BIOS and then change your front side bus speed, the latency timings will instantly go up a notch. Similarly, the latency timings on DDR 2 memory can be much higher than standard DDR memory, though this is more than made up for by the memory's higher bandwidth. Instead of adjusting latency, you'll arguably get a larger performance boost from overclocking your memory, which we'll cover next.

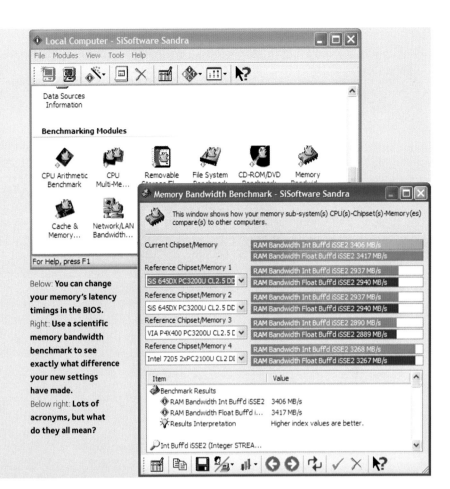

Below: **You can change your memory's latency timings in the BIOS.**
Right: **Use a scientific memory bandwidth benchmark to see exactly what difference your new settings have made.**
Below right: **Lots of acronyms, but what do they all mean?**

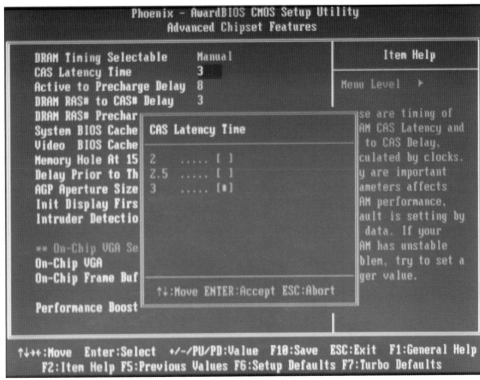

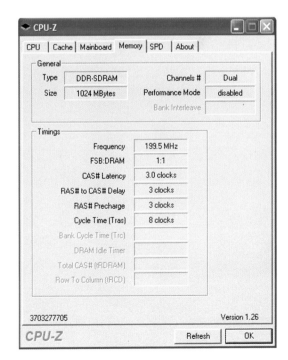

Overclocking your memory

> Your computer can only go as fast as its slowest part. There's no point having 677MHz dual-channel memory if the front side bus only runs at 533MHz.

As with overclocking your CPU and graphics card, overclocking your memory is a simple matter of increasing its clock speed. However, it's not quite as simple as increasing the megahertz. You'll also need to consider the speed of your motherboard's front side bus or HyperTransport speed.

Think of this as Henry Ford's production line, where the chain of workers can only go as fast as the slowest member. It's the same with a computer. There's no point in having your memory running at 667MHz and then setting it in dual channel mode, if your processor's front side bus is only 533MHz—you'll simply end up creating a lot of extra heat for no real purpose.

The key to this is to run your memory synchronously with your computer's front side bus or HyperTransport (i.e. at the same speed). Let's take the example of a Pentium 4 with an 800MHz quad-pumped front side bus. The physical front side bus speed will be 200MHz, so PC3200 DDR memory (which also has a physical speed of 200MHz, doubled by DDR technology) in dual channel memory mode, which doubles the bandwidth again, will be all you need. This is the exact reason why extreme memory is for overclockers only.

You can, of course, run your memory asynchronously with the front side bus, and either have faster memory than the rest of the system, or a faster CPU, but there really is very little point to this and the performance gains will be minimal.

So, if you've had the foresight to invest in some high bandwidth memory for overclocking, as well as some decent cooling for your CPU and motherboard's Northbridge, you should be able to overclock your memory synchronously with the rest of the system. In the BIOS, this is often written in the form of a ratio, and if you have some decent overclocker's memory that goes to the speed of your overclocked

CPU's front side bus, then you should be able to overclock your memory synchronously.

How you actually do this in the BIOS will vary from board to board. Some will just overclock the memory at the same time as the front side bus speed, while others let you set a ratio for the memory speed to the front side bus speed. Others, meanwhile, let you change the multiplier for your DDR memory so that it's 1.3 or 1.6 times as fast, instead of double. In all cases, you want the speed of both your memory and the front side bus to be the same. If you need to, pull out your calculator and do the math.

Once you've done this, save the changes and exit, then see if your system boots into Windows. If it does, then run a benchmark to ensure it's still stable. If it isn't, or if Windows never loads, then your memory either can't handle the speed or it may just need a bit more power. As with the CPU, you can usually help it out (if your BIOS will allow it), by taking the voltage up a little bit. Once you've changed this, try the boot up and benchmark procedure again and see if you have any more success.

If you don't, then it's worth increasing the voltage of your motherboard's Northbridge too—it might be struggling to handle the increased front side bus speed without more power. If your BIOS allows this, and your components aren't heating up too much, then it may just be that your parts need more power. Try taking the voltage up a notch (or two) and see how this works.

When your system's stable, run your benchmark again to see how much faster it is. As with all overclocking, it's a game of hit and miss, and you need to just keep trying various settings until you get the speed you want. You don't want to be restricted by one part of your system when overclocking, though, so having memory with low latency timings and high bandwidth headroom can really help out here.

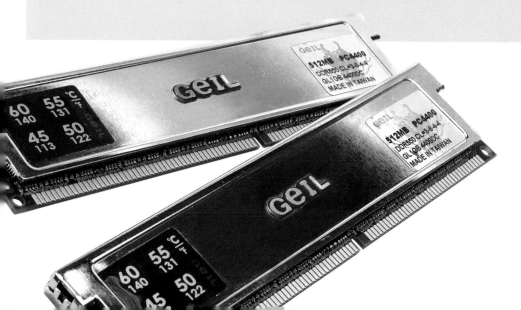

Right: Make sure that your memory is running synchronously with your machine's front side bus speed.

Below: Dual channel memory will double your bandwidth, but it's only worth doing this if your processor and motherboard can run at that front side bus or HyperTransport speed.

Below right: Give your memory more voltage if your system fails—as always take things slowly, one notch at a time.

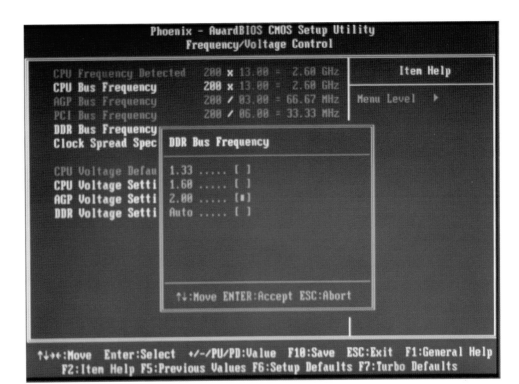

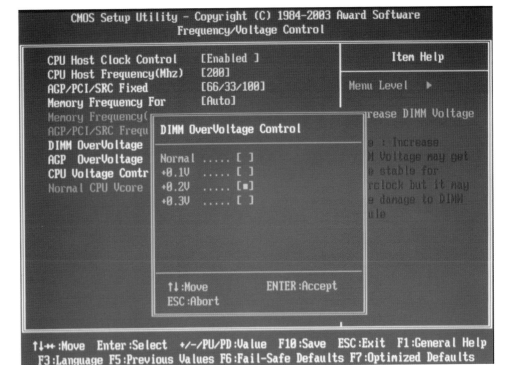

120 > 121

Overclocking your graphics card

> Don't expect a huge speed increase from overclocking your graphics card. You might be able to run games at a few extra frames per second, but it's no substitute for a full upgrade.

If you're into 3D games, then the next part of your PC that it's worth overclocking is your graphics card. If your graphics card is based on an NVIDIA GeForce GPU, you can even overclock it directly from the Display properties. You can access these by right-clicking on your Windows desktop, clicking on Properties, choosing the Settings tab, and then clicking the Advanced button; your graphics card's settings will be under the tab with the little NVIDIA logo on it.

In order to access the overclocking settings, you'll need to enable a handy little feature that NVIDIA appropriately calls "Coolbits." This is a part of the driver that NVIDIA likes to keep secret from users who might accidentally break something, but if you know what you're doing, it lets you perform some great tweaks on your graphics card. Coolbits is actually inside every NVIDIA ForceWare graphics driver; you just have to enable it. All you need to do is download the file coolbits2.reg (just run a Google search on it), double click it and select "Yes" when Windows asks if you want to add it to the registry. After that, you'll find a whole new load of goodies in your Display properties, including a Clock Frequency Settings section for overclocking.

ATI has yet to introduce manual overclocking in its drivers, but if you have an ATI Radeon card, it's worth going to www.techpowerup.com/atitool and downloading the ATITool utility. This gives you everything you need to overclock your card.

There are plenty of third-party software utilities that will do the job equally well, including Power Strip (available from www.entechtaiwan.com/ps.htm) and RivaTuner (available from www.guru3d.com/rivatuner). All you need is a program that lets you alter your graphics card's core (the graphics chip) and memory clock frequencies.

Once you have access to these settings, your first step is to find out how fast your graphics card's

memory will run before it starts to flake out. Start by taking the card's memory speed up by a modest amount (say 4MHz), apply the settings and then run a graphically intensive benchmark (see page 122). If the benchmark runs fine, with no graphical glitches (look for strange flashing squares or dots appearing), then take the memory speed up another notch. Keep repeating this process until your benchmark either freezes up, or starts looking like multi-colored static. When it eventually gives up, just take the memory back to the speed setting you had it on previously, run the benchmark again just to make sure that everything is okay, and hey presto, that's your memory's overclocking ceiling.

Now keep your memory at that setting, and repeat the process with the core clock speed. Eventually you will find a setting that's stable, faster, and (best of all) completely free.

Bear in mind, though, that this is the way to manually overclock your card. Both NVIDIA and ATI now offer automatic overclocking features for some cards in their latest drivers. These will automatically overclock your card's core and memory a bit at a time until they find a stable setting, which you can then stick with. Unfortunately, this often leads to unstable settings. At the end of the day, you know which games you use with your graphics card, and a driver doesn't, so it's always worth checking your settings with a game you actually play.

Just a word of warning: you can't expect your benchmark results to skyrocket after overclocking your graphics card. You might get an increase of a few frames per second, but the difference isn't going to be huge. Think of overclocking your graphics card as a way to make the difference between a slightly jerky 26fps and a slightly smoother 32fps in a 3D game. It might make the difference between a playable and unplayable frame rate, but it's not going to do the same job as a full graphics card upgrade.

Right: **When you start seeing glitches such as these bright green patches, then you've overclocked your card too far.**

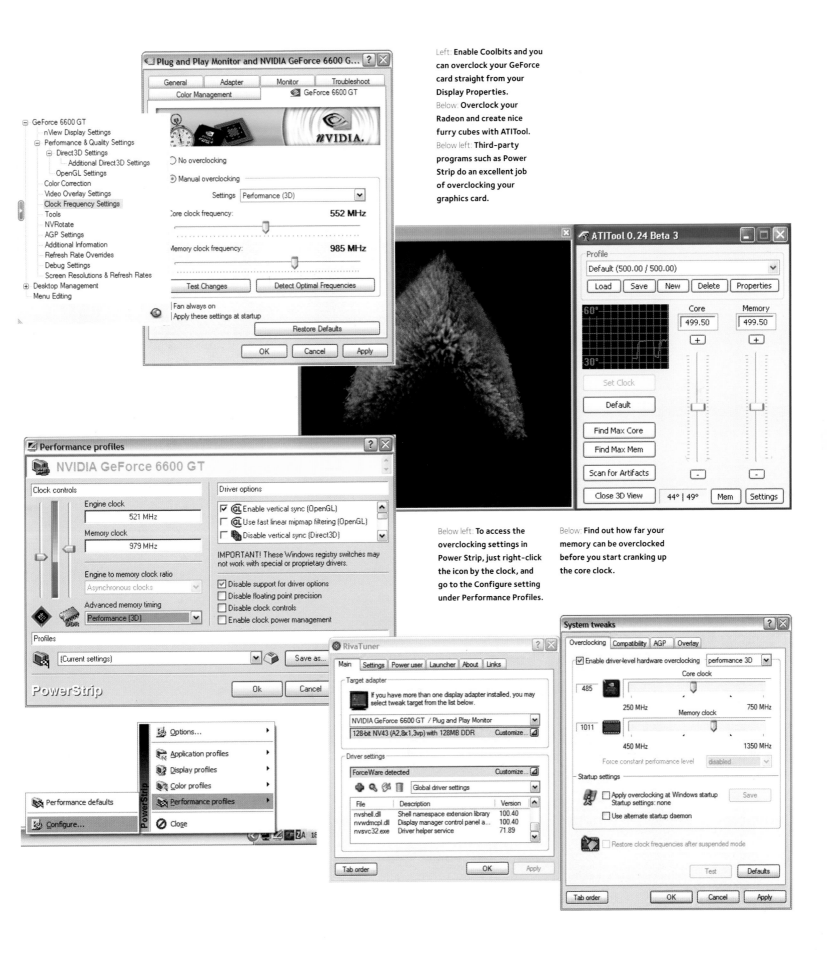

Left: **Enable Coolbits and you can overclock your GeForce card straight from your Display Properties.**

Below: **Overclock your Radeon and create nice furry cubes with ATITool.**

Below left: **Third-party programs such as Power Strip do an excellent job of overclocking your graphics card.**

Below left: **To access the overclocking settings in Power Strip, just right-click the icon by the clock, and go to the Configure setting under Performance Profiles.**

Below: **Find out how far your memory can be overclocked before you start cranking up the core clock.**

122 > 123

Making your mark

> Benchmarks are a minefield of controversy, and hardware manufacturers will sometimes tweak drivers to give better results.

You may want to make your PC faster for a genuine reason, but there's no disputing that the PC enthusiast scene is the techie equivalent of a soapbox derby, which isn't necessarily a bad thing. Still, there's no point in overclocking your PC to the extreme if you don't have something to show for it.

This is where benchmarks come in. A benchmark is simply a test run by your PC to show how well it's performing. Coming in many varieties, the benchmark world is also a minefield of controversy, where hardware manufacturers often seek to destroy the reputation of a benchmark (sometimes providing drivers that cheat) if it gives their product bad results.

A lot of this can be taken with a pinch of salt, but there are some important factors to consider when benchmarking your PC, and the first is how realistic your benchmark is. Many commonly used benchmarks, such as FutureMark's PCMark04 and 3DMark05, are synthetic, meaning that they run their own software to simulate how your PC performs particular tasks. These can be good for getting a score that's directly comparable to another PC, but they don't tell you how fast your PC is at running real programs.

This brings us on to the next type of benchmarks, which are commonly known as "real world" benchmarks in the industry. These use real programs, such as Adobe Photoshop, running a series of scripts through them, doing the types of things that people actually do with their PCs. Real world benchmarks are widely considered the best way to test your PC, as they actually tell you something useful as well as giving you a performance score.

To stress all the areas of your PC you'll need to select a range of real world benchmarks. A photo-editing test, for example, is good for pummeling your memory, but a video-editing test is good for hammering your hard drive, and an audio encoding test can really push your CPU. You will also want to test the things that you actually use your PC for. There's not a lot of point in having a PC that's really fast at applying filters in Photoshop if you never actually do any photo editing.

The same dichotomy applies to 3D games, and there are plenty of ready-made synthetic benchmarks, as well as ways to benchmark real 3D games. It's up to you to choose an appropriate balance to tell you what you need to know.

While we're here, it's also worth mentioning the third type of benchmarks, called component-based benchmarks. These tests are a kind of middle ground, using their own proprietary software with components from real applications. One example of this is the SPECviewperf benchmark, which uses the renderer from 3ds Max to realistically simulate a 3D rendering workstation, without you having to pay thousands of dollars for 3ds Max. However, these tests are only really relevant to the workstation industry and the press, rarely testing anything relevant to the general home user— whether you're an enthusiast or not.

Over the next few pages we'll go through some real world and synthetic benchmarks, for both 2D software and 3D games, which you can use to benchmark your PC, giving you a gauge of how fast your machine is, as well as a score that you can use to see how your creation measures up.

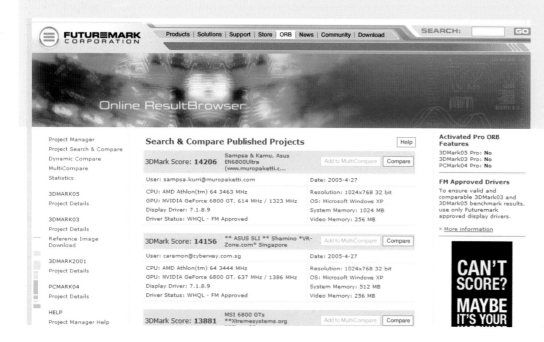

Left: **Use benchmarks to prove just how fast your PC really is. If you make it the top of the leader board (or even into the top 100) then you've done seriously well.**

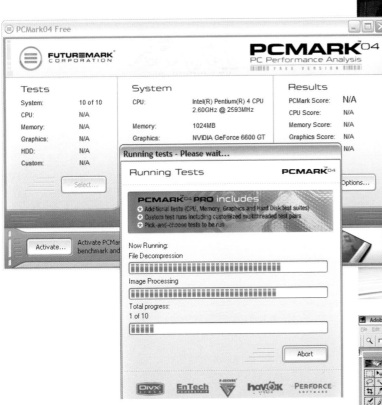

Right: **FutureMark's famous 3DMark05 and PCMark04** are great for generating scores, but they don't tell you how fast your PC will be when running real games.

Right: **Real-world** benchmarks test the speed of real applications, such as Adobe Photoshop, but they're only worth using if you actually use that software.

Below left: **Benchmark real games** such as *Far Cry* to see how fast your PC is in the real world.

Below right: **Component-based benchmarks** like the SPECviewperf just benchmark a part of an application, such as the renderer from 3ds Max.

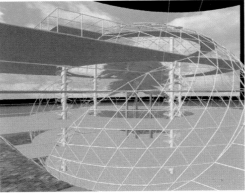

124 > 125

2D benchmarks

> The problem with all synthetic benchmarks is that they don't give any indication of how fast real-world applications will run.

The golden rule of benchmarking is that it's always best to test software that you actually use while it's doing things that you actually do. However, as both a point of comparison and a gauge of performance, synthetic benchmarks also have their rightful place in the world of benchmarking. Another good use for synthetic benchmarks is that they can often use hardware features that "real" software hasn't caught up with yet. Of course, there's a fair argument that says this is irrelevant, but synthetic benchmarks can give you an idea of how quickly your PC could perform in the future, while demonstrating that your hardware's features are all working properly.

Besides, many synthetic benchmarks are free to download and can be run in seconds, so it's not as if you've got anything to lose. One prime example is SiSoft Sandra (downloadable from www.sisoftware.net), which comes with a suite of scientific tests for your individual components. Sandra is ideal for showing the difference in MFLOPS (millions of floating point operations) between CPUs, as well as how much memory bandwidth you've got. Real software is unlikely to show a difference between a 1,066MHz and 800MHz front side bus when it comes to memory bandwidth, but Sandra will. Not only that, but Sandra also comes with a menu of different systems' scores so that you can see how your PC measures up.

Another popular synthetic benchmark is FutureMark's PCMark series. PCMark04 runs a series of virtual tests that simulate how quickly your PC performs

certain tasks, such as grammar checking and audio encoding. PCMark will also give you a score at the end, which is comparable to other PCMark scores. However, unlike Sandra, the free version of PCMark doesn't tell you anything scientific that real-world benchmarks can't (although the Professional version allows you to run some memory benchmarks and hard drive tests). More importantly, it also doesn't tell you how quickly real software will run. Your MP3-encoding software, for example, could be optimized for certain CPU instructions, which PCMark's isn't, and vice versa.

FutureMark's real-world equivalent of PCMark is SysMark. This runs a series of tests using real software, and the 2004 version includes full Microsoft Office application tests, as well as McAfee's VirusScan, Macromedia's Dreamweaver, and Adobe's Premiere, After Effects, and Photoshop. The only problem with this, of course, is that you have to license the software, and it isn't cheap. In fact, SysMark 2004 currently costs $399.95, which is all well and good for big businesses, but not so great for the individual user.

SysMark's history hasn't been without controversy—its popular 2001 version was often criticized for favoring Intel processors. Of course, it's arguable that maybe Intel's processors were just faster, but as AMD wasn't a member of the Bapco consortium (the consortium of computer publications and hardware manufacturers that produce FutureMark's benchmarks) it gave the cynics some reason to be skeptical.

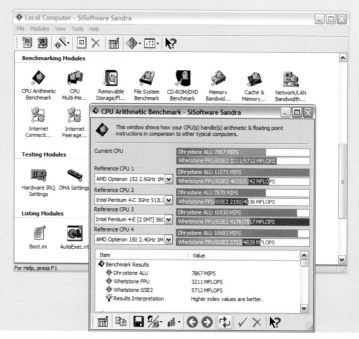

Left: **See exactly how CPUs differ with Sandra's CPU benchmark.**

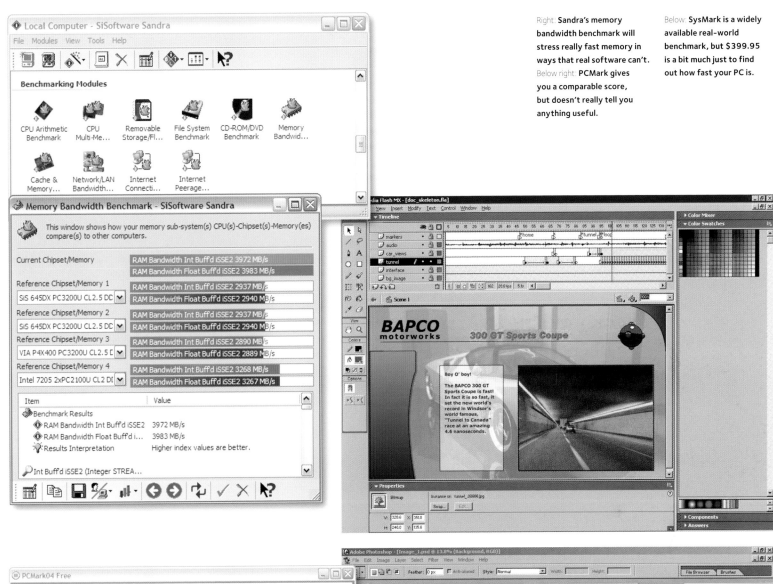

Right: Sandra's memory bandwidth benchmark will stress really fast memory in ways that real software can't.

Below right: PCMark gives you a comparable score, but doesn't really tell you anything useful.

Below: SysMark is a widely available real-world benchmark, but $399.95 is a bit much just to find out how fast your PC is.

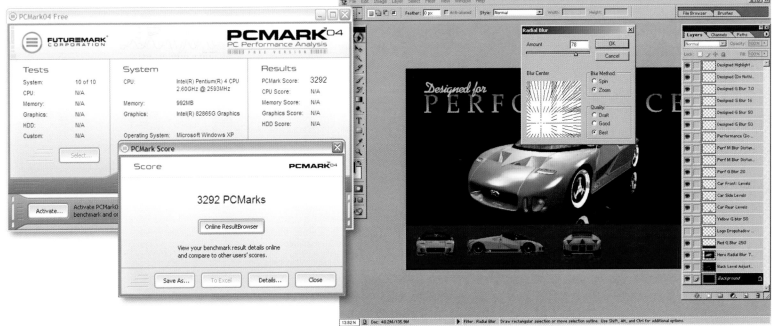

2D benchmarks 2

> It's good to have a series of tests that stress different parts of your system—video encoding for your processor, Zip compression for your hard drive, and so on.

Just because the commercial real-world benchmarks are out of reach doesn't mean that all real-world benchmarks have to be. To add to the collection of benchmarking software you already own, you can also download free demos of many other applications.

As mentioned, the best form of benchmark is one that tests a software package that you really use, one that really slows down your PC. Think about the hardcore computing tasks that force you to sit around twiddling your thumbs while your PC ploughs through them. After that, all you have to do is make a test that can be consistently repeated and then time it with a stopwatch. Instant benchmark.

Examples of things that can be consistently tested could be encoding the same set of WAV files into WMA files, converting the same MPEG-2 movie into DivX format, or zipping up the same 1.3GB of files with WinZip. Once you've got a repeatable test, you can then run it again after any upgrades and see if it's made your real-world task any quicker.

This is why it's also good to have a variety of tests, all of which stress different parts of your computer. Video and audio encoding tests, for example, are going to really push your processor to its limit, while a Zip compression test is going to pummel your hard drive. Also, if you have a copy of Adobe Photoshop, you could run a batch test

(select Batch from the Automate part of the file menu), and time how long it takes to apply the same filters to lots of large images. Depending on the images, this could stress your memory as well as your hard drive.

The only downer about this method is that you'll have no point of comparison other than your own records. However, if you use freely downloadable demos then there's no reason why your friends can't use the same benchmarks too. Free versions or demos are available of WinZip (www.winzip.com), dBpowerAMP Music Converter (www.dbpoweramp.com) —which converts audio files—as well as VirtualDub (www.virtualdub.com) and TMPGEnc (www.tmpgenc.net) —which convert video files. There's also a free demo of Corel Paint Shop Pro 9 available (www.corel.com), which could be used to test photo editing features for free.

The only drawback to this method is that it doesn't test future features (in fact, it often acts as if they aren't there), and also doesn't give you the same huge comparable database of scores that widely available benchmarks have. This is why it's good to have a mix of both, especially when you can do it for free. Test the future proofing of your setup and see how fast it theoretically is with Sandra, and then see what real impact your upgrades will make using real software in real-world tests.

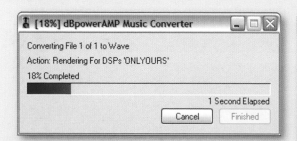

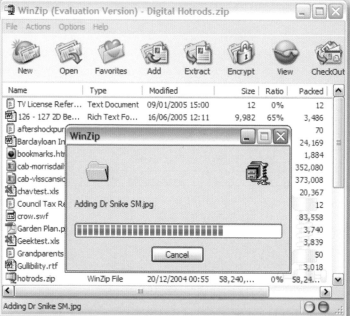

Far left: **To test your processor, convert the same audio files and time how long it takes.** Left: **A compression test with the freely available WinZip will really hammer your hard drive.**

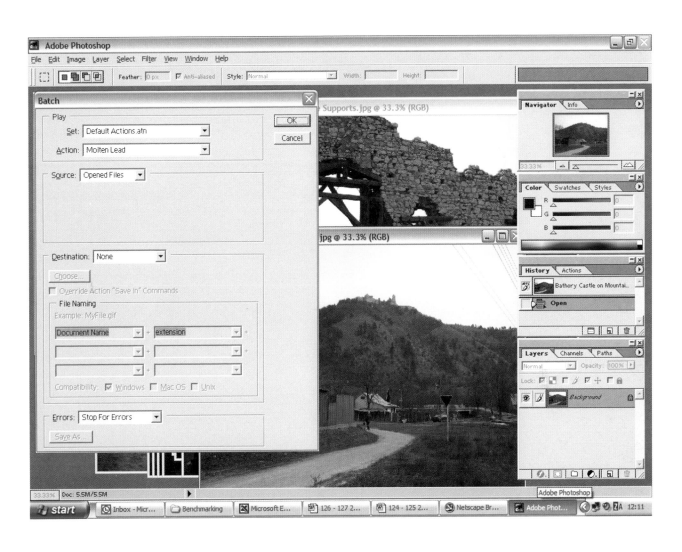

Above: **Time how long it takes to apply the same filter to a batch of images in Photoshop.**

Left: **Virtual Dub is a piece of video capture/processing software that can be set to batch process a series of video files and really stretch your processor.**

128 > 129

3D benchmarks

> Arguably the best 3D benchmark is FRAPS, which can record the minimum, maximum, and average frame rates of any game.

Thankfully, it's much easier to get comparable real-world benchmarks in 3D games. This is because most graphically intensive 3D games have a standard benchmarking utility built in, which will test the same portion of a level while simulating gameplay.

There are two main ways that benchmarks in 3D games work, and the first is with a "timedemo." This is where the computer races through a recorded demo as fast as it can and times how long it takes, recording the average frame rate in frames per second (fps). The other method is to run through a recorded demo in real time, as you would if you were playing it, while calculating the frames per second as it runs. This is how the *Far Cry* demo benchmarks run.

The first method is the one used in most of id Software's games, such as *Quake III Arena* and *Doom 3*. It's not realistic in the sense that no one would ever play a game at the speed high-end cards can run it, but it does show you what your hardware's capable of. In the case of *Doom 3*, it's also worth noting that the game itself is capped at 60fps (as the game's world doesn't refresh at more than 60Hz), so any frame rates higher than that in a timedemo will be meaningless in terms of realistic gameplay.

The way that you get most of these benchmarks to run is through the game's console, which you can usually access by tapping the "~" (tilde) key (in *Doom 3*, you have to press Ctrl, Alt, and ~ simultaneously). Once you see the console, you then have to type in the command to run a demo, followed by the name of your demo. For example, to run the default *Doom 3* timedemo, you bring up the console, and then type in "timedemo demo1." This method varies from game to game, but some research on the Web (or even your game's readme file) should be able to help you out. After the demo has run, the average frame rate will then be displayed, either in the console or in a pop-up screen.

There is an easier way to do it, which is to use the 3D benchmark automation program Bench'emall (www.benchemall.com). The idea behind this package is that it can automatically run benchmarks through several games, while you go off and do what it is you like to do other than overclocking. In order for you to actually do this, you would either have to illegally crack all the games you were benchmarking (use an illegal third-party hack that forces the game to run from the hard disk without the CD in the drive), or install a separate CD drive for each game's disc. Obviously, neither approach is ideal.

Above: **Use FRAPS to record your frame rates while you play.**
Right: **It can also demonstrate your current frame rate in any game (that's the yellow number in the corner).**

Even so, it still offers an easy-access route into standard benchmarks. All you have to do is click on the game you want to benchmark in the panel on the left, point Bench'emall to your game's location on your hard drive, select the settings you want benchmarked and then hit the stopwatch button.

If you can, it's also a good idea to cache a timedemo first. This will stop it stuttering on the second run (where the frame rate is actually recorded from), and will give you a better idea of your PC's maximum horsepower. Again, the way you do this varies from game to game, but you'll be able to find out how with a bit of research. In *Doom 3*, for example, you add the command "+precache 1" to the Command line parameters in Bench'emall to force it to do this.

Arguably the best way to benchmark a 3D game, though, is with a little utility called FRAPS (www.fraps.com), which you can run while you're playing a game, and it records your minimum, average, and maximum frame rates while you play. The best things about FRAPS are that you can run it in any 3D game, it shows you the frame rate you'll actually get in real games, and it also gives you a frame rate in any part of a game you want.

Left: **Bench'emall makes it easy to benchmark games without learning all the console commands.**
Below: ***Doom 3* is capped at 60fps in the game, so any frame rates in the timedemo over this are meaningless in terms of real world testing.**
Below right: **Bring up the *Doom 3* console by pressing Ctrl, Alt, and ~ at the same time. Your frame rate will appear after the timedemo has run.**

130 > 131

3D benchmarks 2

> One problem with 3D benchmarks is that they can become CPU limited, and not give a true indication of the speed of your graphics card.

When using FRAPS, It's also extremely useful to have the three frame rate measurements, as, while it's the average frame rate that's most often quoted, it's also interesting to see your PC's lowest frame rate. The generally held view is that a game needs to be running at a minimum of 30fps to fool the human eye, and if your minimum frame rate is well below this (even if the average isn't) then your game isn't going to be fluidly playable all the time. Ideally, you want to aim for a minimum frame rate of around 30fps, with an average of around 45fps to get the best from your game.

One major thing to look out for in 3D benchmarks, though, is that they can become CPU limited. Basically, your graphics card can only process the data handed over by the CPU. Left waiting for data from the CPU, the graphics card is far from full capacity. The upshot of this is that if you're testing graphics cards with the same CPU, you won't see any difference between cards, whether they're really powerful or not.

This usually happens in comparably undemanding benchmarks at lower resolutions, but it's starting to happen more and more at higher resolutions (even with anti-aliasing and anisotropic filtering turned on) especially with high-end graphics cards and dual-graphics setups. In a way, this proves a point—that a high end graphics card doesn't make a lot of difference to today's 3D games—but it can also be avoided by using a more demanding benchmark. One example is in *Far Cry*, where the standard Fort demo benchmark is now CPU limited with high-end cards, even at high resolutions. Alternately, *Far Cry's* Volcano benchmark can still stress a graphics card without being CPU-limited.

If you are trying to test a really high-end system, keep your eye out for games that test new features. For example, *Splinter Cell: Chaos Theory* already has a Shader Model 3 mode that takes advantage of the latest features of NVIDIA graphics cards. Meanwhile, the Shader 2.0 ++ mode in *Chronicles of Riddick: Escape from Butcher Bay* uses the latest soft shadowing techniques, absolutely annihilating any current graphics setups at higher resolutions.

As with 2D benchmarks, the problem here is that you're testing tomorrow's hardware with today's software, and just because a high-end graphics card makes no difference to a benchmark today, doesn't mean that it won't in the future. This is another area where synthetic benchmarks can come in handy, and FutureMark's 3DMark series is the most commonly used. 3DMark2000, for example, tested transform and lighting before any games used it, 3DMark2001 tested DirectX 8's pixel and vertex shaders before any games employed the technique, and the latest versions test an enormous amount of features that aren't used to a full extent in current games (if you're wondering what these are, you can get a rundown of what each test is supposed to simulate at www.futuremark.com).

3DMark2000 and 3DMark2001 were based on the *Max Payne* game engine, and therefore also had a real world basis, but 3DMark03 and 3DMark05 are completely synthetic. They do, however, test a lot of new graphics features and will really stress out a graphics card, even at the default resolution of 1,024 x 768. 3DMark gives you a score at the end, which you can then add to the FutureMark leader board to see how your score (often depressingly) compares to others. You can also get a breakdown of the frame rates for the individual tests. The idea of the end score is that it refers to an average frame rate if you divide the score by a hundred (so a 3DMark score of 3,400 means a rough average frame rate of 34fps).

3DMark is a good benchmark to use to see how well your system will cope with tomorrow's games, and it's also free to download a basic version that runs the game tests at the default resolution. However, as with all benchmarks, you need to run a variety of tests to get an accurate picture of how fast your machine is, and many graphics cards are better at particular games than others.

Just because one graphics card is faster in 3DMark05 than another, doesn't necessarily mean the other card is trash. Benchmarks are a great indicator of performance, but they're not the be all and end all. Ultimately, you can't test every single thing that your PC does, and even if you could, it wouldn't be an accurate portrayal of how different people use their PCs.

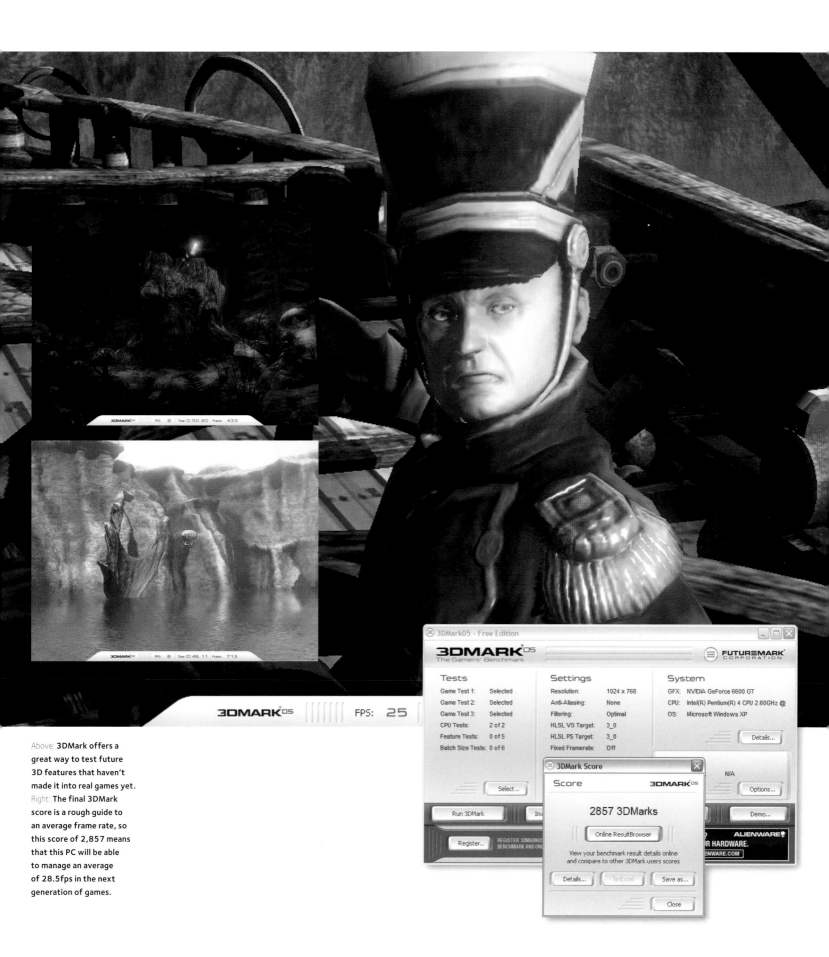

Above: **3DMark offers a great way to test future 3D features that haven't made it into real games yet.**
Right: **The final 3DMark score is a rough guide to an average frame rate, so this score of 2,857 means that this PC will be able to manage an average of 28.5fps in the next generation of games.**

134 > 135

Voodoo Omen Extreme Gamer

> Voodoo claims that it goes "beyond the other PC makers when it comes to delivering extremely insane personal computers."

The Omen is proof that not all PCs are created equal.

Although these photos of the Voodoo Omen look absolutely amazing, they still don't do justice to what, in my opinion, is the most impressive power-PC ever built. Seeing this PC in the flesh (so to speak) is also pretty dangerous, as it instantly makes you consider taking out various loans and new credit cards in order to buy one for yourself. You can't help feeling that your impending bankruptcy is what the "Omen" in its name refers to.

At a gulp-inducing minimum cost of $5,050, saying that the Omen isn't cheap verges on stating the obvious. It's also fair to say that you could build yourself a similarly specified system for much less money, but it would take months to build something that looked half as good, and you would need access to some pretty impressive machine-cutting equipment, too. Voodoo modestly calls its system-building skills a "balance between art and science," while the company's website says that you're only welcome to browse through its systems "if you feel truly worthy of the noble heritage of the Desktop or 'Tower' style PC."

So what are you paying for here? Well, there's the fully customized case. Voodoo hasn't just slapped a couple of lights into a Cooler Master Wave Master case and called it a "custom PC." Instead, they've modded a Lian Li PC-V1000 beyond all recognition. The front panel has been replaced with one of Voodoo's own design, and the whole exterior has a beautiful finish that Voodoo calls "BAM" (brushed, anodized, and machined). Not only that, but the case has also been drilled full of vents to let as much air in as possible, and it has some beautifully machine-cut designs and sensibly placed red and white lights and LEDs all over it. Available in ten colors, the

Omen is also customizable to your requirements if the morbid black color scheme isn't to your liking.

But that's just the outsides, and the insides are just as tasty. The system's cables and the water cooling system's tubes have all been routed and placed neatly with incredible attention to aesthetics, and the specs are absolutely awesome. You've got a choice of either AMD or Intel dual-core processors, two GeForce 6800 Ultras in SLI configuration, and a particularly beefy 600W power supply to run it all. Plus, the water cooling system cools absolutely everything through four waterblocks— one on the processor, one on each graphics card, and one on the motherboard's Southbridge.

Normally, this kind of outlandish specification would mean that your PC makes more noise than a windfarm during a hurricane, particularly with two dual-slot GeForce 6800 Ultras, but the Omen's water cooling system puts a stop to this. The Omen is actually surprisingly quiet in use, which is mainly because its radiator has two large SilenX 120mm fans, and a third at the back acting as an exhaust fan.

The Voodoo Omen is today's ultimate PC, and it's priced accordingly. But if you've got the money, you're not going to find a better crafted, ready-built enthusiast's PC. Voodoo claims that it goes "beyond the other PC makers when it comes to building and delivering extremely insane personal computers, but then that is the very reason why we exist." It's hardly a humble statement, but given the evidence, it certainly seems to be true.

If you're feeling particularly affluent, then visit www.voodoopc.com for more details on this PC, as well as the company's many other custom-built designs.

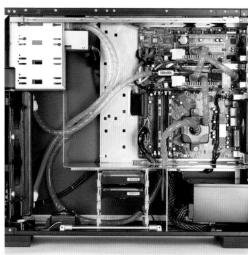
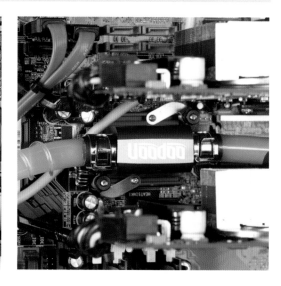

Alienware Aurora 7500SLI

> Alienware PCs have started to become well known and trendy, and "true" geeks don't like this very much.

Alienware's space age case has become an icon of PC enthusiasm. The *Star Wars* version comes in both light and dark side versions, although I have no idea why on earth you'd choose the light side.

If the twisted sci-fi artist H. R. Giger had designed Darth Vader's helmet, then it would probably look a bit like the front of this instantly recognizable Alienware PC case. In fact, this is probably part of the reason why Alienware decided to produce a Star Wars edition of the Aurora, available in both light and dark side editions after *Episode III: Revenge of the Sith* was released.

Some see Alienware as the main instigator of the enthusiast trend, or at least the first company to be really adventurous with its case design, and Alienware is often the first name that comes to mind when you think of enthusiast PCs. You'll also find that some of the more elitist people in the scene turn their noses up at Alienware, but that's mainly because Alienware PCs have started to become well known and trendy, and "true" geeks don't like this very much.

This is a shame, as Alienware makes decent machines. The inter-galactic company has two main product lines: the Area 51, which uses Intel processors, and the Aurora, which uses AMD processors. Both use the same sinister Alienware full-tower case, which looks fantastic, and you're simply not going to get that case from anyone else. The eerie glow that shines through the grille looks really cool, you get a choice of otherworldly colors, from "Conspiracy Blue" to "Space Black" and the glowing alien heads on the outside are a great touch.

Unlike the Voodoo Omen (see page 134), the wow factor isn't quite so active once you get inside. The PCs are tidily built, but there's none of the jaw-droppingly gorgeous lights, and no water cooling system either. Alienware offers some potentially serious specs, though,

including SLI graphics (with an appropriately hefty 600W Enermax PSU), an 800GB hard drive setup (using two 400GB hard drives in RAID 0 configuration), and a dual core Athlon 64 X2 4800+ processor if you've got the money for it. The spec is also widely customizable to your own needs. However, I'd advise you not to bother with the dual GeForce 6600GT SLI option. This is really for people who want two graphics cards for the sake of it, and you'll get similar performance (and less noise) from a single 6800GT, not to mention an upgrade path with the ability to add another graphics card later if you want to.

Of course, the downside to this kind of spec, especially with two graphics cards, is that it all needs plenty of cooling, and with no water cooling system, all the Alienware Aurora machines that I've used have been frustratingly noisy. Thankfully, though, they've also been very fast and well put together.

Obviously the price depends very much on the system you order, but you can get a decent machine for under $3,000. You could, of course, get a significantly cheaper model with similar specifications elsewhere, but it wouldn't have this fantastic case, and Alienware also has an impeccable record of customer support. Alienware is a highly exclusive and well-respected brand, and the company knows this, boldly stating that its PCs offer "high performance, superior build quality, innovative style, and award-winning support." It depends on your priorities really, and if you're after a high-speed gaming machine in a great-looking, unique case and aren't bothered about noise, then you can't go far wrong with an Alienware Aurora.

138 > 139

Dell Dimension XPS

> There's virtually no hot air inside the case, so the fans can spin at a much lower speed. For an air-cooled high-end system, the XPS is unbelievably quiet.

If you need any more proof that PC enthusiasm is becoming a mainstream hobby, then look no further than the Dell Dimension XPS. Some see this as an invasion of their world, a bit like the corporate sponsors of major music festivals, but I actually find it very flattering to think that what was once a minority interest is now being taken so seriously. This hasn't been an easy transition for Dell, though, and its first few XPS systems had some problems.

The first was a lack of understanding of the target audience. The XPS Gen 3, for example, came with a choice of either a pitiful Radeon X300SE or an extreme (for the time) X800XT Platinum Edition, with no other choices in between. What's more, this early effort was impossible to overclock, with all of the options that you wanted to get to frustratingly grayed out in the BIOS.

Thankfully, though, Dell has learnt its lesson, albeit gradually, and you'll be able to overclock a dual core 3.2GHz Pentium D 840 Extreme Edition CPU in the XPS Gen 5's BIOS to 3.4GHz and 3.6GHz. However, that's still the limit of your overclocking options, so you can forget tweaking your CPU's voltage to get a few more clocks out of it. To a certain extent, this is understandable. Not only does Dell want to keep the number of potential support issues down to a minimum, but it also doesn't want to upset its biggest business partner, Intel. Even so, this is a brave step for Dell, which historically has frowned upon user intervention.

These days, you're still limited to a choice of two graphics cards, although the entry level GeForce 6800 is more respectable than a Radeon X300SE, and the Radeon X850XT PE option will be great for anyone who wants high-speed gaming. There's no option for dual graphics, though, and this lack of flexibility is what separates the Dell XPS from other enthusiast machines.

This is a shame, as the machine itself is actually pretty good. Dell makes a big fuss about the fact that you can change the color of the bezel's backlight, but what's really interesting is the design of the case inside. Dell has paid an enormous amount of attention to keeping things quiet, and the 460W power supply sits in a separate part of the case at the bottom, which keeps its hot air out of the rest of the case. The CPU has a similar system, with a massive green plastic duct shifting all the hot air straight out of the back through a 92mm exhaust fan. The upshot of all of this is that there's virtually no hot air inside the case interfering with the cooling of components, so the fans can spin at a much lower (and thus quieter) speed. In fact, for an air-cooled high-end system, the XPS is unbelievably quiet.

Okay, so having a PC with Dell on the front of it isn't particularly cool, but this is a well-designed computer and it's great to see that the big corporations are starting to take a serious interest. Not only that, but the XPS isn't ludicrously expensive, either.

Left: **The new Gen 5 XPS offers basic overclocking features, although they're still very limited.**
Right above: **If corporate giants like Dell are producing enthusiasts' PCs, then we know we're on to something.**
Right: **You can change the color of the backlight behind that front shield to any one of eight colors. Exciting, huh?**

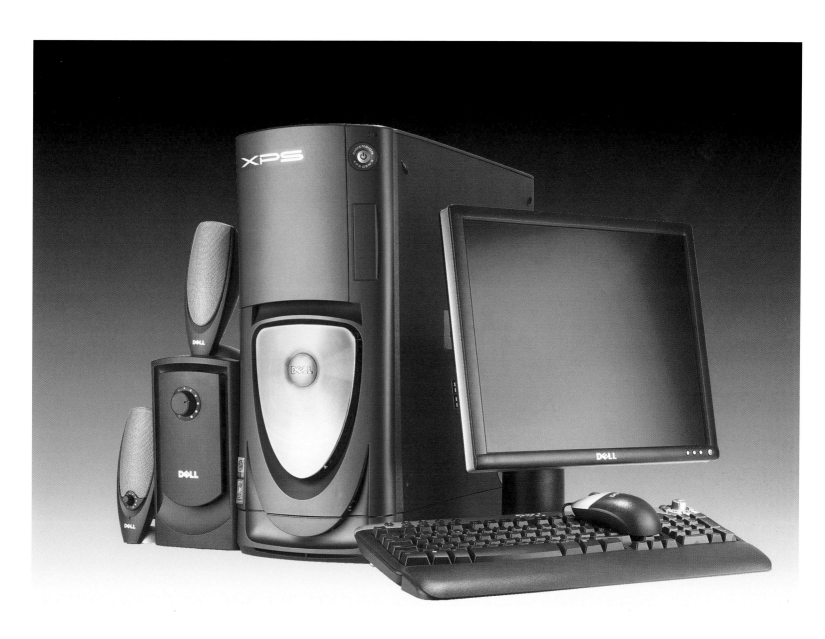

Real Machines RX1

> The PC has been built into Asetek's standard VapoChill case, which is about as attractive as an elderly walrus

In October 2004, Intel officially pulled the plug on the 4GHz Pentium 4, saying that it was going to increase the performance of its chips by other means. You can understand why, but you only need to see the amount of fuss made about the millennium to see that humans just love big round friendly numbers. You might not have been able to tell the difference between a 3.8GHz and 4GHz Pentium 4, but it would have been a great status symbol. However, you can still get to 4GHz with a bit of overclocking, and it's an even bigger status symbol when it costs $7000 and has a refrigeration system attached to it. That's precisely what the UK-originated Real Machines RX1 is: a 3.6GHz Pentium 4 overclocked to 4GHz with a VapoChill phase change cooler.

Asetek's VapoChill system is perhaps the ultimate CPU cooler, being able to take the surface temperature of a CPU down to -40˚F (-40˚C). However, that's about all it does, which is great for getting a processor running stably at 4GHz, but (unlike a standard water cooling kit) it still leaves the rest of your components a little hot under the collar. Real Machines gets round this with a range of options. The standard setup is to have a VapoChilled CPU and a water-cooled graphics card and Northbridge, but these can also be air-cooled to save you a bit of money.

The PC has also been built into Asetek's standard VapoChill case, which was specifically designed to

hold the VapoChill cooling system, and is also about as attractive as an elderly walrus. Thankfully, though, Real Machines has managed to hide this with an absolutely incredible paint job. You can, of course, get it without the paint and knock $180 off the price, but why would you, when Real Machines' chromatic "Color Flip spray" paint job looks so good? There's a choice of "aquamarine" and "cascade copper," both of which mix a gorgeous range of colors together, and look highly reminiscent of a TVR sports car, subtly changing color and shimmering as the viewing angle changes.

They will even apply the same paint job to the Logitech keyboard and mouse, as well as the 20in Eizo TFT monitor, so that you get a complete matching set, although you can knock $1300 off the price if you choose not to take the monitor.

Otherwise, the specifications are also suitably high end, with a primary 144GB drive being made from two 74GB Western Digital Raptors in RAID 0, along with a secondary 200GB Seagate Barracuda 7200.7. The specification is highly customizable, too, with a huge choice of alternative graphics cards and processors, and you can also get an Athlon 64-based SLI system if you really want the fastest PC out there. All of which means that you can still get a decent spec VapoChilled system from Real Machines for well under $7,000.

With its VapoChill refrigeration system, the RX1 can easily support a 3.6GHz Pentium 4 overclocked to 4GHz
Above right: **Real Machines' website looks almost as flash as one of its machines**

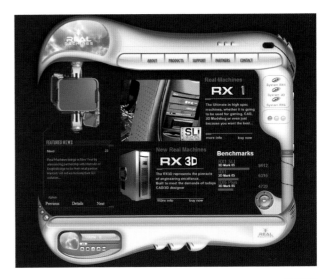

142 > 143

DIGN X15e

> Everything has to be done in a strict order—the motherboard first, then the optical drive, then the PSU and then the HSF for the CPU—or it simply won't fit.

Given the phenomenal success of the Apple iPod, the beloved gadget of geeks and music lovers alike, it's a mystery why there are so few hard drive-based music players to fit into your stereo system. Surely an easy-access hi-fi system, where you just touch the cover of the record that you want to play, or put your whole collection on random play, would be an instant success?

Apparently not. We may have to wait for the usual hi-fi suspects to come up with a decent hard drive and touchscreen-based music box, but PC enthusiasts can get in on the action right now. The answer is already here, in the form of the DIGN X15e aluminum PC case.

The case is big enough to accommodate a full-size ATX motherboard and power supply, along with full-height PCI and AGP cards, plus it also comes with a remote control and 7in touchscreen which connects to your graphics card via a pass-through cable at the back. Surprisingly, it's mainly being marketed by retailers as a media center PC, although why anyone would consider watching *Star Wars* on a 7in TFT is beyond me. What this case does provide, though, is a perfect hi-fi PC that you can proudly display in your existing rack (it even conforms to the standard width specification) and have the convenience of your whole music collection at the touch of a button (or screen, if you will).

Of course, nothing this good comes without a catch, and there are two in the case of the DIGN X15e.

The first is the price. At $950, this case is only for people who really want a hi-fi PC. You could buy a touchscreen, a Dremel, and an aluminum case to mod for half that, although it wouldn't be nearly as convenient. The second major catch is that trying to build a PC into this kind of space is harder than assembling toys on Christmas morning.

It's in the nature of the design that everything is placed so close together, but it really isn't easy. Everything has to be done in a strict order—putting the motherboard in first, then the optical drive, then the PSU and then the HSF for the CPU—otherwise it simply won't fit. Provided you're prepared to do this, though, there's room for a lot of kit inside. As well as the full-size motherboard and PSU, you also have room for up to three 3.5in hard drives (good for lots of compression-free audio), a 5.25in optical drive, and there's also a front-facing 3.5in drive bay underneath a flap, which is perfect for a small fan controller to keep the noise down.

There's no need to build a super-fast PC for playing your music on, so your priority with this machine should be to get a good compromise between speed and fan-noise. Use a minimal passively cooled graphics card and a decent CPU (to speed up MP3 encoding) and you'll be fine. For this reason, you'll also want to avoid putting a fan in the 80mm hole in the back—just put a grille over it to prevent too much dust from getting in to the machine.

Above: **A remote control is
included with the case.
The X15e will look
comfortably at home
with any full-size stereo
system. Why hasn't anyone
thought of this before?**

144 > 145

The small form factor PC

> A small form factor PC is likely to start falling over if it's got a power-hungry GeForce 6800GT and a Pentium 4 Extreme Edition inside.

Personally, I hate the phrase "small form factor." It's one of those stupid pieces of computer jargon like "solutions" or "value-driven functionality" that marketing types like but which mean absolutely nothing to the average person on the street. If they called them something simple like "mini PCs," as Apple did with the Mac Mini, they'd probably take over the high street. Unfortunately, small form factor (SFF) PCs have yet to really take off in the PC world, which is a shame, as they're absolutely fantastic computers.

A common myth about SFF PCs is that they lack the power of a full-size desktop PC. This is true to a certain extent, but it's only the really high-end desktops that they can't compete with. Another myth is that they're all based on low-powered EPIA motherboards; most of them aren't. Not only that, but most of them aren't even restricted to integrated graphics any more. Yes, you really can squeeze the power of a mammoth desktop into a cute little cube.

The idea of SFF PCs has been around for a while, with a few popping up that supported VIA's Mini-ITX platform, as well as some business models such as Hewlett Packard's ePC, but the first company to really generate a buzz was Shuttle with its XPC range in 2001. The idea was that you bought a Shuttle XPC "barebone" system, which came with the case, a specifically designed motherboard, a PSU, and all the cables; you just had to add in the components of your choice. With the ability to take a proper Athlon XP CPU, and even be upgraded via its PCI slot, the XPC was an amazing breakthrough. All that was lacking was support for a decent graphics card, but this was fixed a couple of months later when Shuttle added an AGP slot.

After that, just about every motherboard company under the sun, including MSI, Epox, AOpen,

and Asus jumped on the bandwagon. There's now a whole range of SFF barebone systems that offer an awesome amount of power. What's more, putting a barebone system together is usually easier than setting up a regular self-build PC, as the case and motherboard usually come pre-assembled.

There are, however, some things to bear in mind before buying one, as they do have some serious limitations. The first is the amount of noise they make when they're working hard. This isn't generally a problem if you're using integrated graphics, as the makers of SFF PCs put a lot of work into perfecting the acoustics of the CPU and PSU cooling system. Unfortunately, though, they have no control over the noise that your graphics card cooler will make.

This noise is made worse by the fact that SFF PCs always have their AGP or PCI-E slot right next to the side panel, usually with a PCI slot in between to separate it from the CPU. As you can imagine, putting a sheet of metal right next to a noisy graphics card makes it even louder, and it also makes the pitch higher. Worst of all is that you don't then have the space to fit an alternative dual-slot Arctic cooler.

Another thing to keep in mind is that you're obviously never going to get a full-size PSU into a SFF PC, and the PSUs supplied are usually rated somewhere between 180W and 300W. This is fine for most components, but a SFF PC is likely to start falling over if it's got a power-hungry GeForce 6800GT and a Pentium 4 Extreme Edition inside. You can, however, get a decent compromise with components that are just under the cutting edge ones, as they use much less power. At the moment you can get away with a GeForce 6600GT or a Radeon X800 in a SFF PC, while a 3GHz Pentium 4 or an Athlon 64 3500+ will work perfectly well.

Opposite main picture: **Shuttle's XPC, considered to be the daddy of the SFF PC, now comes in many different styles and colors.**
Right: **Many other motherboard manufacturers, such as Epox, have also jumped on the SFF bandwagon.**

146 > 147

Armari Iwill ZPC64

> You'll have to make compromises. If you want to put a full-size AGP graphics card inside the ZPC64, you'll need to put in a slower 2.5in laptop-sized hard drive.

Huey Lewis & the News once sang that it was "Hip to be Square" and, let's face it, they'd certainly know! But why does everyone assume that mini PCs have to be square-shaped? A part of the reason is undoubtedly that they need a certain amount of space to accommodate a full-size graphics card and optical drive, which is easily done in a cube. Iwill, however, has other ideas, and has shown some ingenious design skills with its super slim ZPC64 barebones system.

By placing a slimline laptop-sized optical drive on its side and putting the graphics slot on an AGP riser that twists it through 90 degrees, Iwill has managed to produce a mini PC that's slim, sexy, and plenty powerful. There's none of the expected messing around with low-performance Mini-ITX boards or integrated graphics in this PC. It'll take a fully fledged 754-pin Athlon 64, as well as an AGP 8x graphics card. Yes, you could actually build a half-decent gaming system in a box the size of a small fan heater.

Of course, you'll have to make some compromises. If you want to put a full-size AGP graphics card inside the ZPC64, then you'll need to put in a 2.5in laptop-sized hard drive, which spins at a slower-than-average speed of 5,400rpm. Even then, you're limited to a graphics card measuring 201 x 102mm, so make sure you know the exact dimensions of your card before making a purchase. According to Iwill's website (www.iwill.com.tw), the ZPC64 will even run

with a GeForce 6800GT, although I wouldn't want to take the risk. You only get a minimal 180W power supply inside the ZPC64, which is going to struggle to produce that sort of power, and there are also the cooling requirements to be aware of—it goes without saying that there isn't a lot of room for airflow inside. I have seen one example up and running with a GeForce 6600GT without any problems, so a half-decent gaming system is perfectly plausible.

I've already mentioned the minimal room for airflow inside the case, so how exactly has Iwill managed to keep this system cool? The answer involves three 60mm fans, and a copper heatsink attached to three copper heatpipes which take the heat to the back of the case. Here, there are a further two heatsinks with copper fins to send the heat into the outside world. It's enough to cool a decent-spec PC, even if it leaves no room for overclocking.

There's even a full range of ports available, including integrated audio (complete with an optical out), and USB2 and FireWire, which are all accessible underneath the stylish front door. This would make it an ideal candidate for a lounge-friendly media center system using a USB2 TV tuner (unsurprisingly, there's no room for a full-size PCI slot inside). This is precisely how Armari is currently selling the system, starting at just over $1800 for an Athlon 64 3000+ media center system, complete with USB2 tuner.

The PlayStation 2 isn't square, so why should your gaming PC be? Amazingly, you can get a half-decent AGP graphics card inside the ZPC64, but only just.

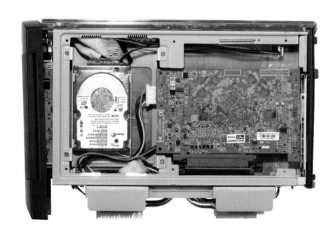

148 ❯ 149

Hoojum Cubit

> The Cubit is only for those with serious money to spend, but if you've got it, there's no better way to flaunt it.

If you're trying to set your home up to look like something from *MTV Cribs*, then the last thing you're going to want is a plain old PC sitting in the corner of your living room, whether it's got an aluminum case or not. If this sounds like you, then it's worth paying www.hoojum.com a visit. Like the gleaming chrome kitchen appliances and onyx coffee table, the works of the UK-based company Hoojum Design are what designers call "lifestyle accessories." Not only that, but they also dispense with the lack of power associated with other lifestyle computers. Called Cubits, they combine specs to die for with looks to pay for.

A Cubit is basically a gorgeous shell (constructed from 5mm aluminum, and then often chrome-plated) built around an intricately designed interior, with a frame of shelves that can accommodate a motherboard, a hard drive, a slot-loading optical drive, and, in some cases, a memory card reader. There's basically a complete PC inside with everything you need, plus you also get a really cool-looking computer to show off to friends, family, and visiting TV crews.

The Cubit started off as a basic Mini-ITX project, using VIA's miniscule motherboards to full effect by producing a tiny PC that had all the basics inside an irresistibly small and shiny box. With its flashy looks, and distinctive swirls cut into the sides, the original Cubit looked awesome, but was dismally slow. This was fine for the average showoff who just wanted a PC that looked cool for word processing and email, but for anyone else, the new wave of powerful PCs based on Shuttle's XPC range (see page 144) looked a much more practical prospect.

Of course, a small company in rural England didn't have the resources to design its own motherboards from scratch, but it did come up with a compromise, which was to buy an XPC, remove the motherboard and then design its own case around it. This eventually became the Cubit P4, finished in chrome so shiny you could even shave with it. With the ability to take a Pentium 4 processor, dual channel memory, and even an AGP graphics card, if you had the money, then there was no reason to stop you buying one.

Since then, Hoojum has produced variations on the theme, with the current flagship being the Pentium 4-based Cubit 5, which can even accommodate two full-size 3.5in hard drives. Hoojum can also build custom variations too, including media PCs with a LCD displays and remote controls, and you can have pretty much anything you want cut into the sides of the case.

Meanwhile, another project that Hoojum has in the pipeline is the Nanode. This is even smaller than the Cubit, and it's based on VIA's supposedly forthcoming Nano-ITX (otherwise known as EPIA N) motherboard range. However, these boards have been "forthcoming" for years, and it's debatable whether they're ever going to see the light of day. It's also fair to say that even if they did, their 533MHz Eden-N processors would make them very slow for all but basic PC tasks, which is a shame as the Nanode looks incredibly tasty.

Tempted to buy a Cubit? Believe me, we all are. Unfortunately, exclusive looks don't come without an exclusive price tag. A Cubit 5 with a Pentium 4 currently goes for a minimum of $2400, which is a long way off the price of a similarly specified Shuttle XPC system that would be just as fast, and would still look quite respectable. The Cubit is unfortunately only for those with serious money to spend, but if you've got it, there's no better way to flaunt it.

Below: **The chrome Cubits are so shiny you could deflect lasers with them.**
Right: **This poor cat ran out of lives after waiting years for VIA's Nano-ITX boards to show up.**
Left: **Have any design you like cut into the case. This one comes courtesy of Mid-Western homemaker, Nancy.**

nanode

cubit

150 > 151

Armari Z64DW SFF Workstation

> Armari knows that PC enthusiasts have quite a soft spot for dual processor machines, particularly those that can be easily carried to LAN parties.

To the outsider, this PC might look like a Nintendo GameCube with a spray of red paint, but don't let that fool you. Just as the GameCube proved that game consoles didn't have to be black and domineering, so the Iwill Zmaxdp proved that monstrously powerful dual processor machines didn't have to resemble the monolith in *2001: A Space Odyssey*. That's right; inside that cute little box are two 64-bit AMD Opteron processors, not to mention an AGP graphics card too.

It's an ingenious piece of design, and Armari (a UK workstation specialist) got in on the action right away. Of course, seeing as the main market for dual processor PCs is workstations, you can get this PC tricked out with a FireGL or Quadro FX card for the 3D animation guys. However, Armari also knows that PC enthusiasts have quite a soft spot for dual processor machines, particularly those that can be easily carried to LAN parties, so it can also be fitted with just about any single-slot graphics card, from a GeForce FX 5200 to a GeForce 6800 GT.

But don't small form factor systems only have tiny 200W power supplies? Well, usually yes, but not this one. Protruding from the back of this PC is a respectable 300W power supply which offers just enough power to run two 2.2GHz Opteron 248 CPUs, making light work of any software that's optimized for multi-threading.

I've seen this system up and running with two Opteron 248s and a GeForce 6800GT inside, and the PSU seemed to be coping with the load admirably. However, it certainly got hot after a while, which is why Armari can also fit it with two "HE" Opteron processors instead, which are a bit more expensive (almost double the price), but only output 55W each, meaning that the cooling system has to shift much less heat from them.

Speaking of which, the ingenious cooling relies on two 70mm fans in the power supply, which pull the air from two massive copper heatsinks outside. These heatsinks are then connected to the Opterons, which sit side by side, via copper heatpipes.

Of course, you can't expect a system like this to be cheap, but it's not as expensive as you might expect, either. We managed to specify a system with two 1.6GHz Opteron 242s, 1GB of RAM, an XFX GeForce 6800GT graphics card, two 200GB Seagate Barracuda 7,200rpm hard drives, and a Sony dual-layer DVD burner for $3000, which is fantastic when you consider what you're getting, and it's in a cool tiny box, too. Incidentally, if the red isn't to your liking, you can have a "more professional" black or white version too.

If you're not in the UK, you can also build one yourself (or find a comparable system builder). Like the Shuttle XPC, the Iwill Zmaxdp (www.iwill.com.tw) is readily available as a barebone system, to which you can do exactly what you want.

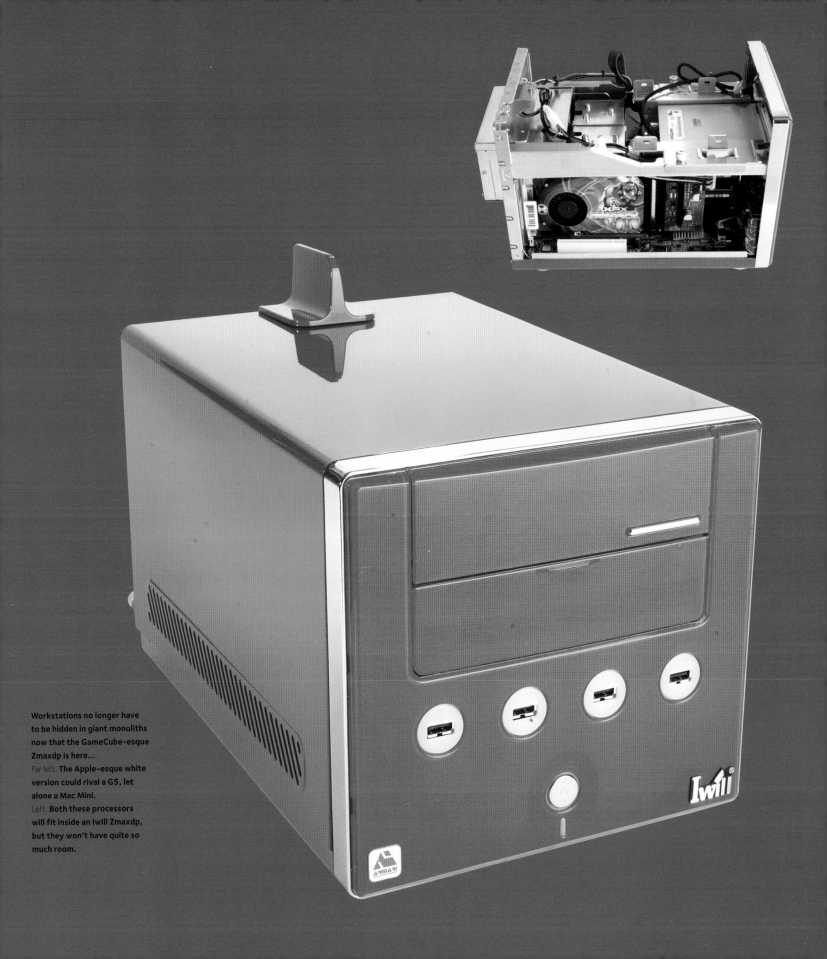

Workstations no longer have to be hidden in giant monoliths now that the GameCube-esque Zmaxdp is here...

Far left: The Apple-esque white version could rival a G5, let alone a Mac Mini.

Left: Both these processors will fit inside an Iwill Zmaxdp, but they won't have quite so much room.

Hush ATX

> The lights on the front are the only way you'll know for sure that it's on. It would be nice to have just one low-speed fan in there to let you know it's working.

With its brushed and anodized aluminum chassis and standard width of 440mm, the Hush ATX will fit perfectly into a stereo rack or even replace a DVD player, which is exactly what it's supposed to do. The point is that it's a PC, but you wouldn't know it by looking at it, and you certainly wouldn't know it by ear.

This is because the Hush ATX doesn't have a single fan inside. In fact, the only time it makes a noise is when you insert a CD or DVD, or when the hard drive makes an occasional chug. Even the latter is kept to a minimum, because the drive is fitted into an anti-vibration chassis.

The way that Hush has done this is so simple that it's amazing no one else is doing it. Basically, the Hush ATX's chassis is a giant heatsink, with massive aluminum fins on either side, linked to all the usual heat-producing suspects with heatpipes. Two of these go to the CPU cooler, one goes to the Northbridge and another one goes to the graphics card. Even the power supply doesn't have a fan, and it still manages to supply 240W, which means that the Hush ATX can also have a pretty decent spec inside.

You can customize this yourself with anything from a 1.7GHz Celeron to an Athlon 64 4000+, or a 2.8GHz Pentium 4. Not only that, but you also have access to a PCI slot and an AGP slot via a riser card, which turns them 90 degrees. This means, of course, that you can also use it as a super-quiet gaming system, without any fans whirring away and distracting you when you're trying to concentrate. However, given the limitation of the power supply, as well as the number of slots graphics

cards can take up, Hush is currently limiting the Hush ATX's graphics options to an X800 Pro, although this is still a very respectable gaming card. Alternatively, you can just use the onboard graphics, and Hush will give you a riser for two PCI cards instead, which would be ideal if you wanted to install a high-end sound card and a TV card at the same time.

As for the rest of the components, the swish drive bay on the front will accommodate an optional optical drive, including a DVD burner, and you can also install up to a 400GB standard 3.5in hard drive, or even two 2.5in laptop-sized hard drives with RAID.

In fact, the only complaint I'd have about this PC is that it really is completely silent. Well, that's the point, obviously, but it also means it's difficult to tell when it's on, and the lights on the front are the only way you'll know for sure. The end result is actually pretty odd, and sometimes you think it would be nice to have just one low-speed fan in there to let you know it's working.

Like performance, the sound of silence comes at a cost, but it's not unreasonable. You can buy a half-decent Hush ATX system on their website for $2480, equipped with a 2.8GHz Pentium 4, an X800 Pro, a 200GB hard drive, a DVD burner, and 1GB RAM.

If you're interested in getting a completely silent Hush ATX PC, which incidentally is available in three colors—silver, bronze, and black—to suit any hi-fi or TV setup, then direct your web browser to www.hushtechnologies.net. In the US, you can also pick up the Hush ATX from www.logicsupply.com.

Right: **The Hush ATX's chassis is a giant heatsink, dispersing heat through these massive fins on the sides.**
Left: **At 440mm wide, it's exactly the right width to fit in with your hi-fi or under the TV. There's a range of colors available to suit every setup—including, bizarrely, bronze.**

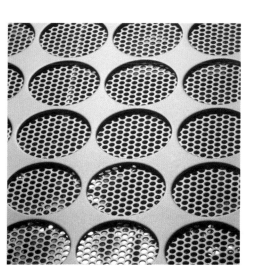

Zalman TNN 500AF

> Make sure you don't undo the work of your motherboard standoffs, as the metal heat-transfer blocks in the case could easily short-circuit a few solder points.

Like the Hush ATX, the Zalman TNN 500AF is a giant heatsink, but you'd need to run it through a car crusher to fit it into your stereo rack. This is because the TNN 500AF is an entirely different beast, built to house a serious PC with no compromises, while still making practically no noise.

Accordingly, the TNN 500AF comes with a hefty 400W power supply to power some serious components, with 20A on the 5V rail, and 18A and 16A respectively on the two 12V rails, delivering enough power for any of today's high-end components. Theoretically, this means you could even put a dual-core Pentium and a GeForce 6800 Ultra into the case. Well, you could, but unfortunately you would need to fit a 120mm fan into the fan mounts to cool them sufficiently.

However, you can safely fit slightly lower spec into the Zalman and still cool it passively. According to Zalman, this means a CPU with a TDP rating of no more than 100W (which means any of the latest Athlon 64 chips, or any Pentium 4 below a 3.2GHz with a Prescott core). You can add any CPU with the addition of a 120mm fan, which, while not completely silent, will still be significantly quieter than a stock cooler. You can say the same for the graphics card—add a fan and you should be OK, but on its own Zalman's specified maximum is a Radeon X800XT PE (this is still an awesome graphics card).

Like Zalman's Reserator, the TNN 500AF's cooling system relies on convection. Hot air rises from the components toward the top, where it's dispersed by two holes for 120mm fans, and another at the back. Meanwhile, cool air is allowed to travel through the bottom of the system to complete the circuit, which can flow in between the case's handy casters and in through another two 120mm holes in the bottom.

Inside the case, just about every component has a block with a heatpipe that connects it to the main case, including the hard drive, power supply, graphics card, and CPU. You also have to fix a few little heat-transfer blocks behind the motherboard to help remove the heat from parts like the Northbridge. Make absolutely sure that you don't undo the work of your motherboard standoffs when you're building a PC inside this, as these metal blocks could easily short-circuit a few solder points on the back of your board if you're not careful.

Basically, you'd have to be really serious about building a silent power house to consider buying the Zalman TNN 500AF. Zalman knows this, which is why it's slapped a whopping $1200 price tag on it. However, you really do get what you pay for. The case's construction is completely solid throughout, and with its casters, hardcore handles, and opening door on the front, this case wouldn't be out of place in a NASA control room, let alone your home. If you want a serious, silent PC, then this is the case to go for. It's seriously expensive, but you're paying for serious quality here. Visit ww.zalmanusa.com for more details, and www.quietpc.com if you're interested in purchasing one.

Right: **The TNN 500AF relies on convection to move air through the bottom and out of the top.**

Left: **Each hot component is prescribed a block with a heatpipe connected to the chassis.**

R2D2

> The only downer with this mod's design is that all the ports are on the bottom of the case, so R2D2 has to lay down if you want to plug things in.

We've recently discovered that R2D2 had the ability to fly with rocket boosters, had been to Tattooine long before he met Luke, and then conveniently had his memory erased just in time to plug several major plot holes. There's no accounting for George Lucas' quality control any more, but somehow R2D2 has come out of the whole experience with some respect still intact, proving he's a resilient machine that can stand up to any number of Tie Fighter blasts and Jawa stun guns.

It's exactly this kind of resilience and stability that you need for a Web server, which is probably one of the reasons why Andreas Bartelt built his OpenBSD Web server into an R2D2 toy. Bartelt bought the toy second hand from eBay, but unfortunately it was one of those very disappointing toys that turns into a completely impractical battle station when you open it up. Bartelt cleared out the model's insides, ready to insert his PC.

Bartelt's main priorities were to make it powerful enough to run everything he needed, but to also make it as quiet as possible. So, with no need for gaming hardware, he based it on a passively cooled 600MHz Mini-ITX EPIA motherboard, and then accompanied it with a silent 60W external PSU.

Even more impressive is the storage system. Bartelt quite rightly knew that hard drives not only make a fair amount of noise, they also get very hot. With this in mind, he decided to put his whole OS on to a 512MB CompactFlash card and plugged it into one of the motherboard's IDE sockets with an IDE to CompactFlash adaptor.

This didn't provide enough space for document storage, though, so Bartelt also fitted an old 20GB Maxtor hard drive in there. As this drive is only accessed once in a while, the machine is still quiet most of the time. Not only that, but Bartelt has also managed to play MP3s on the machine by running a RAM drive that still doesn't access the hard drive, so still keeps the noise down.

The heat issues from the hard drive were resolved by placing it in a bed of blue gel packs, which Bartelt had originally used to cool his cheeks after having his wisdom teeth removed. It's quirky, but apparently it works, helping to take away the heat from the hard drive.

Even so, R2D2 needed a small amount of airflow to extend the life of the components inside, and Bartelt provided this with the quietest 40mm fan he could find, a Papst 412FM, which he keeps in check with a Zalman FanMate fan controller. The fan runs at a slow speed that provides just the right amount of airflow, but is also barely audible, meaning that the machine is still very quiet.

The only downer with this mod's design is that all the ports are on the bottom of the case, which means that R2D2 has to lay on his back if you want to plug things in and out of him, but this isn't a major problem with a Web server, as for the most part it doesn't need a monitor, keyboard, or mouse plugged into it. Far from an overweight blob of grease, this R2D2 is a simple, quiet Web server solution.

Far right: **A single fan provides enough airflow to keep R2D2 cool.**
Center: **Some blue gel packs, previously used to cool his creator's cheeks, take some heat away from R2's hard drive.**
Below: **R2D2 exposes his ports after being hit by a Jawa.**

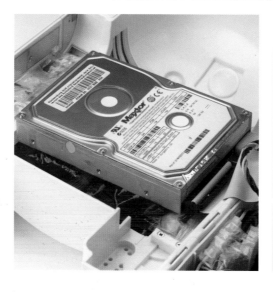

158 > 159

The iGrill

> James had to completely gut all the heating elements from the grill, so unfortunately you can longer cook with it.

Sometimes people get their inspiration from the strangest places. James Goldsmith, creator of the iGrill, is a fine case in point. During an uneventful day in his university lab, he was shown an old April Fool's joke on the website www.thinkgeek.com, showing a fake photo of a "USB 2 iGrill." Most people would just laugh it off as ridiculous, but not James; instead, he felt inspired to build a real one.

A part of the reason was that he wanted a small, quiet server anyway, and had become enamoured with the modding projects on www.mini-itx.com. This provided the perfect excuse to get everything done at one time, and after some internet research, he also found that the 170mm x 170mm dimensions of a standard Mini-ITX board were almost identical to those of the Junior George Foreman Grill.

And so the lean, mean "fat reducing" grilling machine project was underway. James immediately started gathering the parts he'd need for his real-life iGrill, including a purple Junior George Foreman Grill and a VIA CL600 EPIA motherboard. This motherboard is the slowest of a range of motherboards that's not particularly fast anyway, but speed wasn't an issue for this project. The main selling point for this board was that it didn't need any active cooling, which would keep the iGrill quiet. Not only that, but it also came with two 10/100Mbps Ethernet ports, which made it ideal for use as a server or router.

The rest of the spec is made up of 512MB of RAM, an 80GB Seagate Barracuda hard drive, and a 250W Achme PSU, which was designed to fit inside Shuttle small form factor systems. The latter two parts are hidden deep inside the bottom grill plate, although James had to shave a good 5mm off the hard drive with his Dremel to get it to fit. Unfortunately, the same couldn't be said for the PSU, which turned out to be 2cm taller than its official specifications. Undeterred, James dropped it into its place in the bottom grill plate, knowing that you wouldn't be able to see it when the grill was closed (which it would be when it was running).

James' next task was to route the EIDE cables from the hard drive and the power cables from the PSU through a slit that he cut in the molded metal hinge in between the two grill plates. This all went in fine, with the exception of the fat ATX power connector, which also ended up protruding from the bottom grill plate.

Not that it matters. When it's closed, the iGrill looks fantastic, with the motherboard resting neatly under the transparent purple lid, and insulation beneath to stop it shorting out on the metal grill plate.

Of course, James did have to completely gut the heating elements from the grill to fit it all in, so you can no longer cook with it. But then again, we all know that heat and computer components aren't a healthy mix. Since creating the iGrill, James has also had his website (www.igrill.co.uk) listed on www.slashdot.org, resulting in over 400,000 people trying to access the server he hosts on his home ADSL line. Maybe that April Fool's gag wasn't such a ridiculous idea after all.

Opposite, center: **Fortunately, EPIA boards don't get too toasty, even when they're being grilled.**

Opposite, right: **The passively cooled EPIA board keeps the iGrill nice and quiet.**

Below: **You can see the PSU and ATX power connector protruding from the bottom grill plate, but not when it's closed.**

160 > 161

The Windows XP box

> Getting it all in and fixed down required some intricate work, splitting the IDE ribbon cables at every five conductors so they could be slotted into place.

Most creative projects require you to think outside the box, but not this one. Believe it or not, inside this Windows XP box is a fully working PC, complete with hard drive and CD-ROM. The mod's creator, Andy France, wanted a basic server that would always be switched on and didn't take up too much space. It didn't need to have amazing specs, but just enough power to run what he wanted.

This involved a 1GHz EPIA M10000 Mini-ITX board, 256MB of RAM and a 12GB laptop-sized hard drive. This was all then packed into a sleeve that Andy constructed out of a DIY material called Wonderboard, which Andy chose because it's easy to cut. Getting it all in must have been like the computer-component equivalent of Tetris. It's amazing that he managed to make it fit at all, but it's a tight squeeze, and there's probably not enough room to swing a flea inside—there's less than 1mm of clearance space between the CD-ROM and the motherboard chipset's heatsink!

As you can imagine, even a Mini-ITX system will start to heat up when there's hardly any room for airflow, so Andy also put a lot of thought into solving this problem. As the CPU fan sucked in air from above, he cut out a hole in the case immediately above it, then stuck down some plastic ducting to guide the air out. There are also two exhaust fans on either side of the case to remove as much hot air from the system as possible, and Andy even fashioned his own fan grilles from a metal speaker grille with an angle grinder.

Getting it all in and fixed down required some intricate work, splitting the IDE ribbon cables at every five conductors so that they could be slotted into place. The really ingenious bit about this project, though, is that the PC unit will also go into a Red Hat Linux box. Big deal, you might think, but the cool thing is that if you put it in the Red Hat Linux box it automatically loads Red Hat Linux instead of Windows. How does it work? The PC will only fit into the box one way round, and the other way around for the Linux box. A tilt switch from RadioShack that Andy cleverly wired up to a COM port inside then tells the machine to boot either Linux or Windows, depending on its orientation. It's really clever stuff.

Not only is there a lot packed into this box, but it's also pretty solid. When Andy brought it over to be photographed, it got accidentally dropped, but it still worked afterwards. What's really impressed Andy, however, is that over 350 websites have made a link to the page on www.mini-itx.com about the project, and at one time it was even ranked sixth on a Google search for "Windows XP."

Far left: **Put it in the Windows box and it boots Windows; put it in the Red Hat Linux box and it boots Red Hat Linux—ingenious!**
Left: **A tilt switch from RadioShack is wired to the COM port to determine which OS to boot.**
Below: **You wouldn't get much more inside here.**

162 > 163

Project Guitar

> Gutting a small form factor machine can be an ideal compromise between space and power, although it could also end up as an expensive workaround.

The real beauty of this modding project is that it's a PC that works perfectly well as a guitar. Of course, guitar aficionados might be able to tell the difference, perhaps even say it doesn't have the same tone, but the fact that it still works as an acoustic instrument is testament to some fine modding skills. When you're modding a bizarre object into a PC, the real art is getting it to work as both a PC and the original object. Not always easy.

At least a guitar offers plenty of space to play with, and this meant that the guitar PC's creators, Graeme Whaley and Hannah Howson, could build a half-decent PC inside it too. Basically, the modding duo had decided to build a guitar PC as a showcase piece for a guitar festival, but they only had a day and a night to build it. The modding alone was quite a challenge, but this added a little extra pressure.

It also meant that they had to buy all the parts as quickly as possible, and a frantic search was conducted to get it all together. Not only that, but they didn't want to build a PC with low specs, which ruled out using a Mini-ITX board. In the end they settled on gutting a small form factor Athlon XP machine, removing its motherboard. This is sometimes the best thing to do with a modding project, providing an ideal compromise between space and power, although it could also end up being an expensive workaround.

Graeme and Hannah then completed the specs with an Athlon XP 2400+, 512MB of RAM, a 120GB hard drive, and a DVD-ROM and CD-RW combo drive.

They decided to stick with the onboard AGP graphics provided, though, as this wasn't going to be a gaming PC.

After that, it was time to build it, and they needed to take care with this too. A few rushed and jagged cuts and the whole thing would look like it had been modded by a chimp with a saw. Thankfully it didn't, but only due to a lot of careful work, reaching deep inside the guitar. Apparently, fitting the DVD-ROM drive to its space at the far end was an absolute nightmare.

Even so, the job got done, and very good it is too. The small form factor motherboard is ideally placed at the bottom of the guitar, which doesn't interfere with the basic look of the instrument, and you can easily plug cables in and out of it when it's on a stand too. Even the cooling system has been well thought out, with three blue LED fans, complete with protective fan grilles mounted on the back; and, of course, the soundhole at the front of the guitar.

The whole project is completed by a custom-made metal plate on the bottom to hold the motherboard port backplate in place, and there's even a small pair of speakers inside, hooked up to the integrated audio. There's a blue cold cathode light, which along with the blue LED fans, gives the guitar a fantastic blue glow. And in case you were wondering, they did get it finished for the guitar festival, working into the early hours to install Windows on it. That's dedication for you. See www.moddedpc.co.uk for more details on Graeme and Hannah's other modding projects.

Left: **The blue LED fans add a classy look and also help keep the system cool. After all, wood doesn't mix too well with heat.**

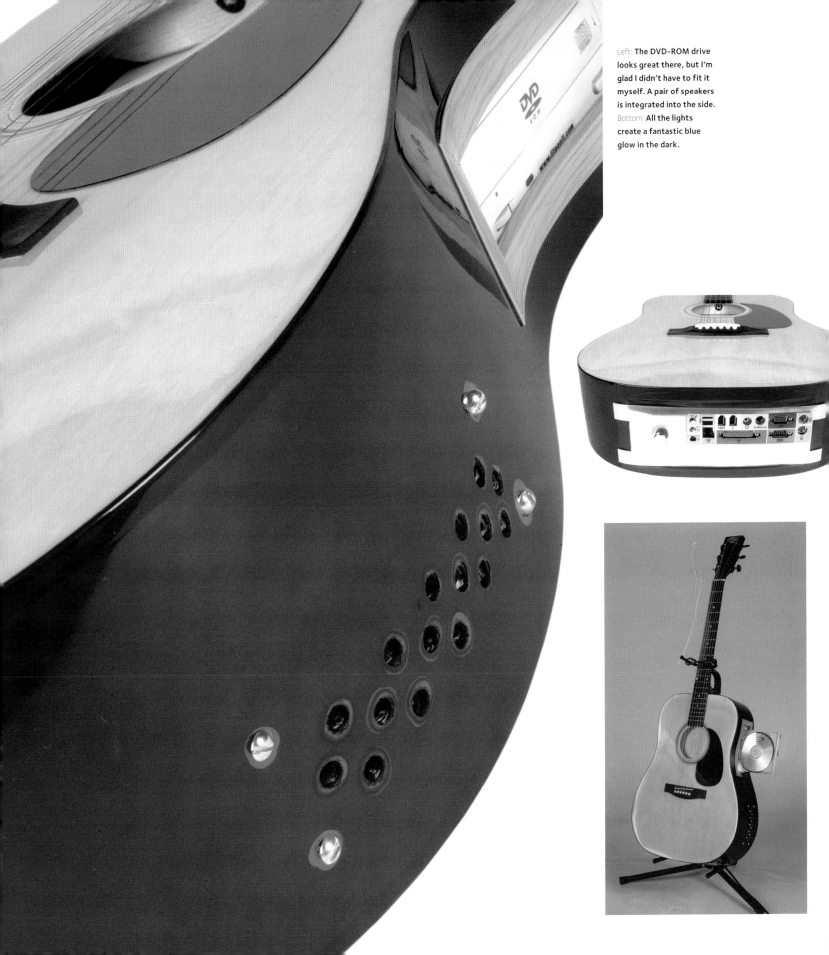

Left: **The DVD-ROM drive looks great there, but I'm glad I didn't have to fit it myself. A pair of speakers is integrated into the side.** Bottom: **All the lights create a fantastic blue glow in the dark.**

164 > 165

Project Sinclair PC200

> The PC200 was my family's computer back in 1988, and I defended it with fanatical ferocity in the face of my friends' vastly superior Amigas.

I'm fairly sure you won't have heard of the Sinclair PC200, which is probably because it was garbage. The original machine (which was actually built by Amstrad) came with an 8MHz AMD 8086 processor, no hard drive, and a hideous, four-color CGA graphics card. Worst of all, it was virtually impossible to upgrade, with just two eight-bit ISA slots that required you to have the lid permanently open to install anything into it. It was, however, my family's computer back in 1988, and I defended it with fanatical ferocity in the face of my friends' vastly superior Commodore Amigas.

In fact, I was so devoted to my trusty companion throughout my teens that I recently decided to gut it and give it the upgrade it deserved. This meant that I not only wanted it to perform like a modern-day powerhouse, but I wanted it to behave like my old computer, too—with the original integrated keyboard and Sinclair joystick.

The joystick wasn't a problem, as it used a 15-pin gameport connector that you can still get USB adaptors for, but the rest of the machine was much more of a challenge. I wanted to use it as my day-to-day PC, which meant that I needed more power than a standard EPIA board, so I decided to gut a small form factor system (the Epox Mini Me) and use its motherboard and power supply in the PC200. The main reason I chose the Mini Me was because it had a front panel with PS/2 ports on it, which I knew I could move inside and plug in the cable from a new keyboard.

Unfortunately, the original keyboard had a proprietary connector, and my knowledge of keyboard wiring and membranes didn't stretch to a re-wiring job. Instead, I dismantled an old IBM keyboard with a Dremel and fitted that inside the PC200's shell. I also used a Dremel to gut out all of the plastic pegs and borders in the chassis, as well as cutting up a VHS video box to make the backpanel for the motherboard. You'll notice that the back (as well as the top lid) also features a light-up Sinclair logo, which I made by printing out the logo on overhead projector transparency film, sticking a few of them together and then illuminating them from behind with a red cold cathode light.

By the end of it all, I had a 3.4GHz Pentium 4 with 1GB of RAM, a 250GB hard drive, and a CD-RW and DVD-ROM combo drive, which is so much better than the original machine that it's a bit like comparing a Model T Ford with a Mercedes S-class. Not only that, but the keyboard and joystick work perfectly, and the original power switch still works, too. Plus, the stupid lid that annoyed me before now actually proves quite handy, as I can just open it up to allow more air into the machine (and quiet it down a bit). Obviously, the airflow around the cramped system isn't ideal, and it does get very hot, but it's also completely stable and has never crashed once, even when running Folding@Home.

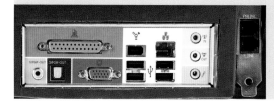

Far right: **The original keyboard was replaced with a hacked up IBM keyboard, which also gives me a Windows key.**
Above: **A Dremelled video box, some OHP film, and a cold cathode light make up the back of the machine.**
Right: **A Matrix Orbital LCD display adds a touch of class that would have made the PC200 a must-have gadget in 1988.**

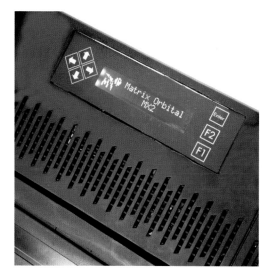

Below: **Sinclair's swan song revamped with some lights, a Pentium 4, and a lot more than four colors.**
Right: **Opening the old lid lets some much-needed air into the system.**

AmmoLAN

> George installed a 6.4in LCD TV to watch movies on. It's worth looking for a VGA input on an LCD screen if you want the picture to be as crisp as possible.

You don't get many geeks on the military front line, which is probably just as well as it would be a surefire way to wipe out our IT support network. Even so, many geeks have a particular fondness for military technology, whether it involves building radio-controlled models of tanks, or watching documentaries about World War II on the History Channel. George Perkins, however, took his interest a step further by building a PC into an ammunition canister, or "AmmoLAN" as he calls it. Well, if you don't like that pun, he could always respond with "Hell, you weren't there, man!"

Puns and soldiering aside, AmmoLAN is a great piece of modding. It certainly helps that George Perkins is a graduate in computer aided design, and accordingly he designed a lot of AmmoLAN's insides using Pro/Engineer (www.ptc.com). This turned out to be particularly useful when he was working out how to get the optical drive into the lid, which obviously needs the correct amount of clearance inside the box in order for the lid to open and close. George plotted this arc using CAD, and then constructed the insides around it. Even the aluminum brackets for mounting the components inside were designed on a computer and then milled by hand.

The .50 caliber can itself is a genuine leftover from the military, which George picked up from www.surplusandadventure.com. George has made it look particularly flashy by integrating a screen and several LEDs and switches on the outside. Apparently, cutting

into the chassis with a Dremel isn't a particularly pleasant experience, though, creating a lot of dust and a nasty smell.

Despite this, George, finished the job and installed a 6.4in LCD TV that he'd picked up second hand in order to display WinAmp visualizations and watch movies. Unfortunately, though, this can only connect to the TV-out on the 1GHz EPIA M10000 motherboard, and it's worth looking for a VGA input on an LCD screen if you want the picture to be as crisp as possible.

Even so, the effect is fantastic, especially when combined with the assortment of 12V LEDs. These LEDs have the advantage of having a resistor inside, which means that you can solder them directly to a 12V output on a PSU without having to solder a resistor to each batch of LEDs. The best part about the LEDs, though, is what George did with them, which was to mount one inside each exhaust vent, making AmmoLAN look awesome when all the lights are out. Similarly impressive is the switchgear mounted on a polished aluminum plate on the lid, with physical switches to flip the system power, eject a CD and switch the LCD screen on and off.

Inside, though, there's a dark secret. While George fixed down a lot of the parts properly, the power supply is only held in with sticky-back Velcro, a material that George says deserves "respect" when it comes to modding. He's right; I also used the stuff to hold the CD-ROM in place on Project Sinclair (see p164). Not that it matters, as it still works fine, and on the outside AmmoLAN is a great-looking mod.

Far left: **These physical switches control all sorts of things, including the LCD screen's power and the eject switch for the CD-ROM.**
Left: **There's a red LED inside each of those exhaust slits, which makes for a great light show in the dark.**

Right: **Well, what sort of movies would you watch on an Ammo can?**
Above: **God bless Velcro!**

168 > 169

Ford Focus

> The minimal EPIA 5000 board came with a 533 MHz processor, onboard graphics, audio, and an Ethernet port. It may not be a speed demon, but it's certainly a fully working PC.

Being a big fan of the World Rally Championship and a PC enthusiast who writes for www.hexus.net, it's no surprise that Gordon Handley decided to build a PC based on a Ford Focus WRC. Inspired by modder BlueSmurf for VIA, who built a Mini-ITX PC inside a model Volkswagen Beetle, he went on to build this superb PC mod.

Interestingly, this isn't based on a complete model kit either. Gordon just bought the shell for the Ford Focus from www.apexmodels.co.uk and then built the rest of the chassis himself. He built the base of the PC from 2mm aluminum which he got from RadioShack, cutting it to the correct shape and size with a Dremel. The wheels, meanwhile, were bought from a local shop and sprayed silver, and Gordon got the tires from an old radio-controlled car. Even the metallic blue paint job is all Gordon's own work.

What's even more amazing is the amount of stuff that Gordon managed to squeeze onboard. Inside that tiny 200mm car shell, there's not only a Mini-ITX motherboard, but also a laptop-sized DVD-ROM drive and a 2.5in 6GB hard drive. These are mounted underneath the motherboard, with spacers inbetween, then connected to the motherboard with the correct laptop-to-desktop IDE adaptors. The DVD-ROM drive is also mounted toward the back of the car for easy access.

The only thing that he couldn't get into the car was, unsurprisingly, a power supply, although he did find an ideal compromise with a 55W Morex external power supply. These external power bricks just connect to a bit of circuit board that you put inside the PC, saving lots of space, and while 55W isn't a lot of power, it's certainly enough to power a low-spec Mini-ITX board fitted with laptop components.

Speed wasn't an issue with this project, but Gordon did want the Focus to be a fully functioning PC. This made a VIA Mini-ITX motherboard perfect for the project. Measuring just 170mm x 170mm, it would fit into the 200mm Focus shell, and it would also offer everything Gordon needed for a PC integrated on to the motherboard. The minimal EPIA 5000 board that he chose for the project came with a 533MHz processor soldered to the board, as well as onboard graphics, audio, and an Ethernet port. It may not be a speed demon, but it's certainly a fully working PC.

The final touch was to add some lighting to the project, not just to make the headlights light up, but also to show off the insides. This involved putting two 5mm white LEDs in the front headlights (connected to the motherboard's power LED header), two red 5mm LEDs in the brake lights at the back (connected to hard drive activity header), and then putting four blue LEDs inside the chassis to light up his handiwork. There are also two switches at the front to switch the machine on and off and reset it. The result is a full-on PC inside a tiny car shell that looks fantastic, and is currently proudly parked under Gordon's TV set. More details about the Ford Focus PC project, as well as Gordon Handley's other modding projects, can be found at www.gordyhand.co.uk.

Left: **The DVD-ROM and hard drive are mounted underneath the motherboard to keep them out of the way. The 533MHz Mini-ITX board may not be fast, but it's very small and has all the necessary features integrated.**
Right: **Gordon spray-painted the shell himself with metallic blue paint.**

170 > 171

Hellraiser

> Chris Dols got on the phone to Hollywood to track down the templates used to make the original Hellraiser box. Believe it or not, he got them.

Based on the dangerously alluring Lemant Configuration puzzle box seen in Clive Barker's *Hellraiser* movies, Chris Dols' Hellraiser PC mod is the work of a true craftsman. He could have easily based the design on a readily available *Hellraiser* toy, but instead he got on the phone to Hollywood to track down the templates used to make the original Hell-raising box in the films. Believe it or not, he got them. Having received his digital copies of the templates, he drew up the plans for this fantastic mod.

There are, of course, three major differences between this mod and the Lemant Configuration puzzle box. Firstly, it doesn't summon up Pinhead and the Cenobites from Hell (at least, not as far as I know); secondly, it has a PC inside it; and thirdly, it's about 100 times the size. In fact, the whole box measures 18in². This is because Chris had an awful lot to fit in to the box, including plenty of stuff from www.cyberguys.com, not to mention a Pinhead action figure and a re-creation of Pinhead's world, complete with red lighting and over 25 blood-spattered hooks (from the local fishing tackle store) and chains hanging form the ceiling.

The box itself, meanwhile, is all built around a pine frame, with pine panels on the outside, two of which can be pulled down to allow access to the creepy world inside. Arguably the most impressive parts of this mod, though, are the intricate wood engravings on these panels. Chris put the markings on by printing out the designs he'd received on a much larger scale and then cutting out the

patterns to make templates. He then attached these to each panel with double-sided sticky tape and sprayed a thin coat of paint over them to mark them out. After that, he used a Dremel with a 1/8in routing bit to rout the markings into the panel. According to Chris, this job took a painful four hours per side, but it was worth it to create the amazing effect that you see here.

To finish it off, he removed the spray paint with some 80-grit sandpaper, and smoothed it all off with some steel wool and 120-grit sandpaper. It then took three coats of oil-based Dark Cherry stain to get the background color of the panels as authentic as possible, along with four coats of brass paint to do the same for the raised patterns, all of which were then finished off with six coats of high-gloss lacquer.

Like Gert Swolfs' HyperCube² mod (see p178), Chris didn't stop at the PC, either. He wanted a matching monitor, too. He achieved this by spraying his old CRT with 20 layers of Dupli-Color Mirage Paint, which changes color depending on which angle you look at it from. To top it all off, it's all cooled by a super-quiet Zalman Reserator water cooling system. Clive Barker would be proud.

Chris is currently in the process of putting together a TV show about modding; see www.modthemachine.tv for more details, as well as www.modthemachine.com for more information about the Hellraiser mod.

Right: **All of that intricate detail was cut out with a router-equipped Dremel. Now that's serious craftsmanship.**
Right above: **Enter Pinhead's world, if you dare, by pulling down one of the side panels. He's got such sights to show you, you know.**
Left: **Chris sprayed an old CRT monitor with 20 layers of Mirage Paint to make it match the puzzle box PC.**
Far left: **It might be about a hundred times the size of the original, but by using the original movie templates, the design is proportionally accurate.**

172 > 173

The Boombox PC

> The dirt-cheap Fujitsu Stylistic tablet PC may only have a 120 Mhz processor, but that's enough to run Windows 98 and play MP3s.

At first glance it would be too easy to dismiss this ghetto blaster PC as one of the usual "crazy" mods circulating the web, another Mini-ITX board wedged inside a gutted gadget from the '80s and called a mod. However, that would be a terrible injustice to the attention to detail in The Boombox PC. Take a closer look at the cassette deck, level meters, and counter in the middle of The Boombox PC. If it's still not clear, look again.

Yep, that's no tape deck, that's a tablet PC displaying an expertly recreated drawing of the original middle parts. Not only that, but the customized MP3-playback software even changes the handwritten label of the "tape" according to the song it's playing. Like many expert modders, The Boombox PC's creator, Greg Dalrymple, didn't stop at the hardware; he manipulated the software too, using MediaCar (a skinable front end for in-car computers) with Windows 98.

The specs inside are pretty unusual too. Rather than buying standard high-spec parts, Greg bought a dirt-cheap Fujitsu Stylistic PC for $80, which he gutted for the project. These tablet PCs only have a 120 MHz processor, but that's enough to run Windows 98 and play MP3s, and they come with a touchscreen, which saves all the hassle of using a mouse to change tracks.

Greg even dismantled the Stylistic's port replicator, taking his soldering iron to the USB header and IPEX plug that connect it to the tablet, rewiring it all to fit the ports into the unit. What's more, he also soldered the Stylistic's audio connectors to the appropriate parts of the original Hitachi TRK-8200HR. So the mic leads go straight to the original microphone, the line-out goes to the boombox's line-in (so the sound still comes out of the speakers), and the boombox's line-in phono sockets are also linked to the Stylistic's line-in for recording.

Greg also replaced one of the screws around the left speaker (which apparently aren't real screws, and are just for show) with a tiny USB webcam connected to an internal USB header, making The Boombox PC a potentially great piece of spy equipment. Not that I'd condone such things, of course.

There's just one problem with taking a piece of junk from the '80s and adding sparkly new bits, and that's that it often ends up looking just that—tricky trash. Greg got around this, however, by filling in all of the cracks (from his hacking, as well as the general wear and tear over the years) with a plastic body filler called Bondo, and then finished off the rest by gradually wet sanding the materials down, polishing them, and then spraying them with metallic car paint.

The result of all this is a fantastic Boombox and PC in one that doesn't look its age and does everything it should do. See Greg's website at www.gutterslide.com for more information on The Boombox PC and Greg's other modding projects.

Far left: **It only has an 8GB hard drive, but that's the equivalent of almost 100 cassette tapes.**
Center left: **The handwritten label changes according to which track you're playing. Really, how cool is that?**
Left: **A secret camera hidden in this screw-hole makes The Boombox PC a perfect way to spy on people.**

174 > 175

Orac³

> Some of the cables were wrapped in Techflex nylon sleeving and surrounded by clear-plastic aquarium hosing.

It's amazing how a child's mind distorts memories. We might remember *Battlestar Galactica* as a *Star Wars*-esque special effects showcase, but when you're confronted by the disillusioning reality of the reruns on cable, you have to wonder if kids' brains are actually filled with some kind of amnesia-inducing custard. The British sci-fi TV "classic" *Blake's 7* is another prime example. You may remember the ship's obtuse computer Orac looking something like this fantastic PC mod, but it actually looks more like a crude Perspex box with a couple of LEDs thrown in.

If only Peter Dickison, the creator of Orac³, had been working for the BBC's special effects department in the late '70s. Taking its name from the aforementioned *Blake's 7* computer and the acrylic C3 case it's built around, Orac³ just goes to show what an inspired modder can do with some time and patience, including three painstaking weeks of planning with good old-fashioned pen and paper.

Believe it or not, Dickison made over a hundred mods to complete the project and had virtually all the insides specially chrome-plated, including the PSU cover, DVD drive covers, a plate to cover the motherboard, and the aluminum hard disk tray. In fact, Dickison even chrome-plated the ABS plastic used in the junction boxes by first covering it in electrically conductive paint.

Orac³ also serves as a fine lesson to us all in cable routing. That Medusa's head of silver snakes you can see inside is actually made from shower hoses, yet still manages to tidy away all the messy ATX power cables while looking high-tech and flashy. Additionally, some of the other cables were wrapped in Techflex nylon sleeving and surrounded by some clear-plastic aquarium air hosing from the local pet shop. The ends of all the cable bunches were then finished off with mono jack plugs and plugged into sockets in the aforementioned junction boxes to link everything together.

Of course, no modding project would be complete without some eerie glowing lights, but Dickison avoided the usual clichéd cold cathode lamps, opting instead for his own green Perspex coverings for the drive bays, made from the same material in between the two halves of the junction boxes, and illuminated from behind with white LEDs. He's also put a funky VFD display behind one bay, along with a fan controller.

To top it all off, Orac³ is even water-cooled. Dickison modded the top of the case with a new panel that he cut out with his jigsaw, sanded down with wet and dry, and then mounted on his two Criticool acrylic reservoirs.

Proof that you really don't need to spend hundreds of dollars at the online overclocking specialist to achieve an amazing effect.

Far left: **Home-made chrome-plated junction boxes link all the cables together.**
Left: **A specially modded top holds the reservoirs for Orac³'s water cooling system.**
Below: **The VFD doesn't serve any real purpose, but it looks really cool.**
Below left: **They might look like parts of a robot, but those silver sleeves are actually shower hoses.**

Right: **The finished article wouldn't look out of place in an adolescent Borg's bedroom.**

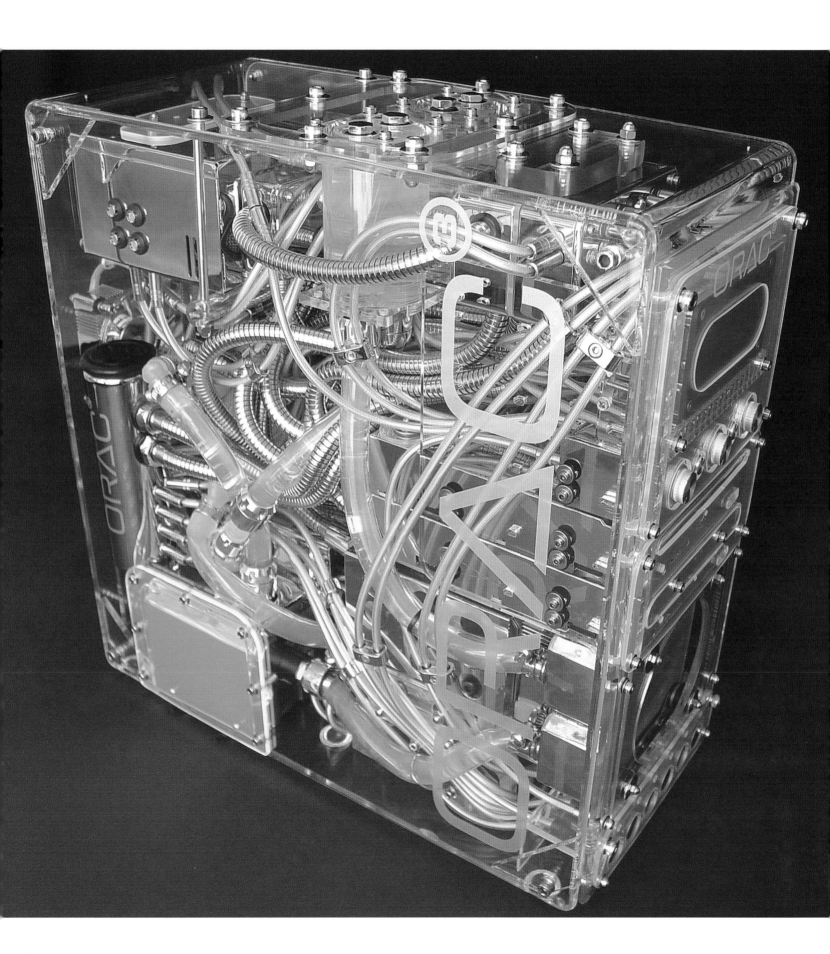

176 > 177

The LAN Truck

> The major attention-grabber is the integrated touchscreen—a 7in Lilliput TFT designed for in-car computers, hooked up to the 12V rail of the Mega PC's PSU.

As a part of the Behemoth team on *Robot Wars* (a TV show in which contestants battle it out with home-made, remote-controlled robots), Ant Pritchard is no stranger to the art of doctoring remote-control models, which is why his PC mod, the LAN Truck, oozes creativity and professionalism throughout the design.

Not only is there a PC inside that Tamiya Mercedes-Benz 1850L 1/14th radio-controlled truck kit, but it still works as a radio-controlled truck too, albeit with a higher torque motor to pull the extra weight. As you can probably guess from the precision of those cuts, Ant didn't sit at home painstakingly cutting those outlines with a Dremel. As a professional model maker by trade, he also owns his own CNC (Computer Numerical Controlled) mill, where the cuts can be programmed on a computer. The result is a PC mod that's so professional looking, it could have been produced in a factory.

However, it's the extra touches that make this mod really stand out. Ant could have just screwed a Mini-ITX board into his truck and called it a PC, but instead he gutted an MSI Mega PC SFF system. This provides the graphical LCD display and buttons on the left, while also providing a half-decent system spec inside—a 2.8GHz Pentium 4, complete with AGP slot, no less.

Of course, the major attention-grabber is the integrated touchscreen. A 7in Lilliput TFT designed for in-car computers, which Ant doctored by soldering on a Molex connector to hook it up to the 12V rail of the Mega PC's PSU. He also machine-cut some new buttons for the screen (one of them even has "LAN Truck" embossed into it), and the screen's original blue backlight shines through to make them stand out even more. What's more, underneath the touchscreen you'll see two Play Station controller ports, as well as two Xbox controller ports, which Ant took from an abandoned Xbox shell, all of which hook up to the PC for console-type gameplay.

The traditional cold cathode lights have also been used to good effect in this mod, with two 4in blue cold cathodes on the bottom, which give the LAN Truck a ghostly floating effect in the dark.

Even the insides have been built meticulously, and planned with airflow and strength in mind. The frame that holds all the parts in place behind the truck was constructed from 2mm aluminum at a local metal workshop, which helps keep everything firmly in place, also helping to move heat away from the components. The polycarbonate backplate behind the truck's rear doors is impressive, too. This has an 80mm LED fan fixed to it to help with airflow, and also has the words "LAN Truck" impressively machine-cut into it.

As a final touch, Ant added a trailer to carry his Logitech diNovo keyboard and mouse, which was constructed from the body of another 1850L truck kit. The end result is a completely self-contained PC mod, monitor and all, that puts most mods to shame. Since building the mod a year ago, the LAN Truck has seen a lot of attention, and has even made it to the Samsung display stand at the CeBIT technology trade show in Hanover, Germany.

See www.makerobotics.com for more details on the LAN Truck, as well as the Behemoth team.

Below: **A CNC mill can achieve a much more professional look than a handheld Dremel, just look at the precision in those cuts.**

Hypercube²

> Hypercube creator Gert Swolfs removed the PSU's case and rearranged the wiring himself to fit it all in. Don't try this at home, folks!

With the possible exceptions of *The Empire Strikes Back* and *Superman II*, movie sequels are generally crushing disappointments that make you feel ashamed to have handed your hard-earned money over to the film industry. *Hypercube*, the sequel to the cult film *The Cube*, is no exception to this rule, but at least its visually distinctive hypercube (a little cube inside a big cube) inspired Gert Swolfs to create this awe-inspiring PC mod, based on his interpretation of how the hypercube's exterior might look.

Looking at all the intricate structural detail in the Hypercube², it's no surprise that Swolfs is an architect by trade. His method is meticulous, with no room for sloppy cuts and jagged edges. Swolfs even designed the HyperCube² in VectorWorks 9, which he also uses at work, so that he could get the precise measurements for laser-cutting the panels.

The whole thing is based around a 274 x 274 x 274mm aluminum frame, which Swolfs had custom-built by a Belgian contractor, with clear and frosted Plexiglas forming the outside walls. Then, just like a real hypercube, there's also a smaller cube inside this frame. This accommodates two hard drives, the PSU and a set of fan controllers, and it also gets all the messy wiring out of the way, while also being easily removable.

At this point you're probably wondering how on earth he managed to fit a PSU inside that tiny cube. Believe it or not, Swolfs actually removed the PSU's case and rearranged the wiring himself so he could fit it all in. He even then went on to metal-plate the insides of the inner cube to avoid any electromagnetic interference. Now that's what I call hardcore modding. Don't try this at home, folks— unless you know *exactly* what you're doing.

Like Orac[3] (see page 174), the Hypercube² also features an ingenious cable management system with plastic tubing and aluminum sleeving (not shower hoses this time), which then terminates the cables with stereo jacks that plug into sockets.

It all adds up to a visually striking PC, which could also qualify as a work of art. The lights also help out, with over 70 ultra-bright LEDs connected to eight different circuits controlled from the toggle switches at the top. These are complemented by three 80mm Cooler Master white LED fans, while a 1.8in Lilliput screen adds an extra touch of sci-fi finesse by showing 3D animations of the case.

As if the PC wasn't amazing enough in itself, Gert Swolfs also modded his monitor to match the design. Hypercube² is an awesome achievement for a lone modder, and there's no way you can do justice to all the work involved in a couple of pages. If you want more information on all the hard modding that went into this creation, check out the full project log at www.bit-tech.net, as well as Swolfs' own site at http://users.telenet.be/hypercube.

Left: **The Cooler Master white LED fans won't be short of friends, with 70 other Ultra Bright LEDs inside the HyperCube.**
Below left: **The HyperCube was planned meticulously, with full plans drawn out using CAD software.**

Right top: **Not even the monitor could escape this modder's intensive project.**

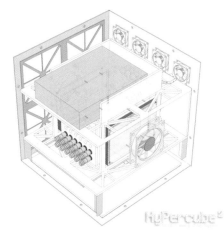

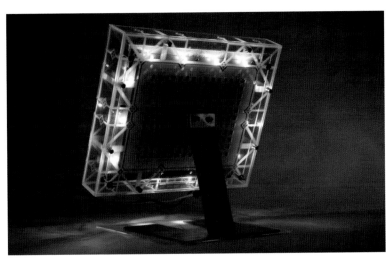

180 > 181

Pink Floyd—The Wall

> The circular window was cut with a water jet cutter. This fires a torrent of pressurized water through a tiny aperture, guided by a computer.

Seeing the marching hammers in Alan Parker's film *The Wall* (based on the Pink Floyd album of the same name) can provoke a whole range of reactions. Some people see them as a terrifying metaphor for Nazi Germany, some see them as a reflection of Roger Water's authoritarian ego, and other, such as Bill Owen, see them as the ideal handle for a Kingwin 242 aluminum case. Having had his vision, Bill sped off to his local hardware store to pick up an appropriately shaped hammer and start modding.

There's no rational explanation for the insane inspiration that's often behind a PC mod, but you can't argue with it when it produces great results such as this Pink Floyd—The Wall mod. Its creator, Bill Owen, mods cases professionally (see www.mnpctech.com for more details), which means he knows some great tips and tricks for getting a great professional finish.

The circular window in the side panel, for example, was cut out with a water jet cutter (see www.customwatercuts.com). These cutters fire a torrent of pressurized water through a tiny aperture that's guided by a computer. It's a very sophisticated process, and it doesn't leave any burrs or jagged edges on your side panel either, which makes it perfect for cutting out intricate details, such as the little hammers in the middle, as well as the 12in circle itself.

The holes for the fan grilles, meanwhile, were cut out with a 4.5in Greenlee die cutter, and the fan grills themselves were cut from plastic styrene and then attached to the metal rings from gutted 120mm metal fan guards. The words "Pink Floyd Inc" were also carved into a block of styrene and stuck to a sheet of clear Plexiglas, which is lit up from behind with a 4in red cold cathode light.

It's the model of the desperate screaming face (originally drawn by Gerald Scarfe) which covers the front intake vent that really stands out. Bill Owen molded this himself with a material called Super Sculpey, a type of modeling clay that remains chip-proof and shatter-resistant after it's been baked in the oven, making it ideal for creating something that looks professional and stays that way. It was then up to Owen's modding partner, Lin Anderson, to airbrush some bricks over the bezel and beneath the window, then paint around the contours of the face to make it look like its skin was really being stretched over the bricks.

Anderson also had the job of airbrushing the superb mural of marching hammers onto the case's other side panel, and it was then up to Owen to put his final touch to the case. This involved writing out the words to the bizarre final song from the Pink Floyd album, "Outside The Wall," onto the top of the case. The letters were cut from red vinyl using a TrueType font called "Floydian" that had been knocked up by a Floyd fan at www.pinkfloydonline.com.

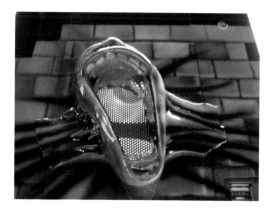

Right: **A sculpture based on Gerald Scarfe's iconic artwork screams out from the intake vent.**
Above: **Hammers make great carrying handles too. No, really.**

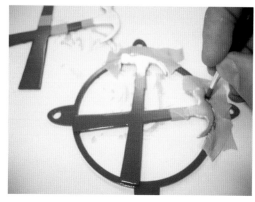

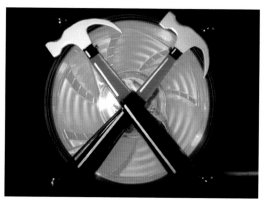

Above: **A water jet cutter provided the crisp cuts to make the excellent window pane in the side panel.**

Right: **These sinister marching hammers were airbrushed on by Bill's modding partner, Lin Anderson.**

182 > 183

AGP—Accelerated Graphics Port. A high-speed slot in your PC for installing graphics cards, now being superseded by PCI-Express.

AMD64—AMD's technology for a 64-bit processor that is also backwards-compatible with 32-bit software.

Athlon 64—AMD's mainstream 64-bit x86 chip, using AMD64 technology.

Athlon 64 FX—an AMD64 chip aimed at the enthusiast, generally with a bigger cache and higher clock speeds than the Athlon 64.

ATX—An old standard format for motherboards, which all use the same 20-pin power connector.

ATX12V—An extension of ATX with an additional four-pin 12V connector. This is mandatory on all Pentium 4 boards, and is also found on older AMD64 boards.

ATX12V 2.0—A further extension of ATX 12V with a 24-pin main power connector and two 12V rails.

AMD64—The umbrella name for AMD's 64-bit technology. Opterons, Athlon 64s and Athlon 64 FX chips are all collectively known as AMD64 CPUs. AMD64 is AMD's technology for running 64-bit code on an x86 processor.

Benchmark—A piece of software used to measure the speed of your PC.

BIOS—Basic input output system. The BIOS is the part of your computer you can access when you press <del> to enter setup when you first switch on your PC. It takes the form of a set of screens where you can change the clock speed of your processor and memory, disable or enable features on your motherboard, and a whole lot more.

BTX—An alternative replacement for ATX from Intel, with an optimized airflow system that only requires one cooling fan for all the components.

CAS—Column Address Strobe. A measurement of memory latency, also known as CL (CAS latency). This is the number of clock cycles that your memory will take to start work on a read command.

Celeron—Intel's budget chip. Celerons are never as quick as the more expensive Pentium chips, but they're often much more overclockable.

Clock speed—The speed that your processor runs at, measured in MHz or GHz. Also sometimes known as clock frequency.

Cold Cathode—The most common type of lights used in PCs, cold cathodes normally come in 4in and 12in lengths.

Core—The chip in the middle of a CPU package that actually does the processing.

DDR—A way of doubling the bandwidth on memory by processing data at the start and end of each clock cycle, effectively doubling the work being done per clock.

DDR 2—Like DDR memory, but requires less power and runs at a lower voltage, which enables it to run stably at higher clock speeds. DDR 2 is used as standard on modern Intel systems.

Dual core—A CPU featuring two physical processors inside one package.

EM64T—Intel's technology for running 64-bit code on an x86 processor.

Frame rate—The number of frames that are displayed per second in a 3D game; you want an average of at least 30fps to fool the human eye.

Front side bus—Carries data between your CPU and the rest of the system.

GDDR3—Fast memory, like DDR 2, that can be easily overclocked and has minimal cooling requirements. GDDR3 memory is often used in high-end graphics cards.

Graphics pipeline—The process of creating a 3D object in a scene, determining its position, and how it will react to other elements.

GPU—Graphics processing unit. NVIDIA's term for a graphics chip that can process transform and lighting calculations as well as rasterize in hardware.

HDR—High dynamic range. A feature that enables a much greater range of lighting in 3D scenes, allowing for great blinding sunlight effects.

Heatpipe—A pipe filled with some kind of coolant that takes heat away from a device and moves it

somewhere else. Heatpipes are often used in small form factor systems to move the heat from the processor and power supply outside the system.

HSF—Heat Sink and Fan. The standard air-cooling devices attached to CPUs and GPUs to keep them cool.

Hyper-Threading—Intel's technology for treating a single processor as two, allowing dual-core style multithreading across a single CPU.

HyperTransport—AMD's alternative to the front side bus, which connects the CPU to the rest of the system.

IDE—The standard connector for hard drives and optical drives for decades. IDE attaches with ribbon cables, but has since been superseded by the superior SATA technology.

ISA—An older expansion slot technology preceding PCI. ISA slots are now completely obsolete.

LCD—Liquid Crystal Display. The most common form of flat-panel display.

Level 1 cache—The closest cache (a small amount of fast memory) to the CPU.

Level 2 cache—A second, and larger, reservoir of cache for storing data that can't fit into the Level 1 cache.

Level 3 cache—A third stage of cache used for larger data storage on high-end server chips, such as Xeons, as well as some Pentium Extreme Editions.

LGA775—Intel's new socket standard for its Pentium desktop processors. The socket is the other way around from a normal socket, with pins rather than holes in the socket, and contact pads on the processor.

Media center—A PC that doubles as a DVD and music player, sometimes also with the ability to record live TV. These are often complemented by Windows Media Center Edition.

MicroATX—A smaller ATX motherboard. MicroATX motherboards will still go into an ATX chassis, but not vice versa.

Mini-ITX—A standard size for the tiny motherboards often used in modding projects. Mini-ITX boards measure 170mm x 170mm and were brought about by VIA.

Mod—To alter a component or PC to your own design, or (as a noun) the result of such an alteration

Molex—The four-pin connector that attaches to AGP graphics cards, and IDE hard drives and optical drives.

Multiplier—The multiple of your computer's front side bus speed that your processor runs at.

Multi-processing—Using more than one CPU in the same PC.

Multi-threaded—Software that distributes its workload over multiple processors.

On-die cache—Memory that is mounted physically on the CPU die, rather than on a separate piece of circuit board.

Opteron—AMD's 64-bit processor for servers and workstations. You can run several Opterons at the same time for multi-processing.

Optical drive—A drive that users a laser to read or write a disc, such as a CD-ROM or DVD burner.

Overclock—Take a chip beyond its standard clock speed.

PCI—The standard expansion slot for cards, including sound cards, modems, and network cards in your PC. PCI slots used to be for graphics cards too, but this job has now been assumed by the AGP and PCI-E slots.

PCI-Express—The new slot for cards, particularly graphics cards, in your PC. The speed of your PCI-E slot is determined by how many lanes it has. Graphics cards are usually allocated between four and sixteen, while standard devices are just allocated one lane.

Pentium—Intel's brand name for its processors.

Pentium D—Intel's new brand for its Pentium 4 desktop processors.

Pentium M—Intel's mobile chip, based on a hybrid of the best parts of Pentium III and Pentium 4 technology. Pentium M chips can also be used in desktop machines, and are acclaimed for offering high performance with minimal power or residual heat.

Phase change—Cooling with a refrigeration system that relies on the "phase change" principle of turning water into a vapor.

Pixel pipeline—Refers to the number of pixels that can be processed simultaneously when a graphics card is running a pixel shader.

Pump—The part of a water-cooling loop that actively pushes the water around it.

Pixel shader—A small program run on a graphics card's GPU to process pixels.

Quad pumped—Intel's latest chips have a "quad pumped" front side bus, so while the actual front side bus is around 200MHz, the bandwidth will be approximately four times that.

Radeon—ATi's brand name for its GPUs.

Radiator—The part of a water-cooling loop that cools the water. Radiators come in varying sizes, and are usually measured in terms of the size of the fan attached.

Reservoir—A part of a water-cooling loop that stores water, including enough for a backup in case of evaporation. Reservoirs can also act as an air trap when your loop is switched off.

SATA or Serial ATA—A new technology for connecting hard drives and optical drives to your motherboard. SATA potentially offers a greater data transfer speed than IDE, and also uses much smaller and neater cables.

SATA II—Like SATA but faster. SATA II devices have a theoretical maximum transfer rate of 300MB per second, but hard drives are never likely to be that fast.

Sempron—AMD's budget range of processor. Was 32-bit only, but is steadily moving to AMD64 technology. You can get Semprons in both Socket A and Socket 754 versions, and the latter are acclaimed for their high overclocking potential.

SFF—See Small Form Factor.

Skinning—Customizing a piece of software to give it a different look.

Slipstream—The process of integrating a service pack on to your Windows installation CD.

Small Form Factor—A mini PC or barebone system.

Socket 478—An older socket for Intel's Pentium 4 CPUs.

Socket 479—Intel's socket for Pentium M processors. Socket 479 motherboards can also take Socket 478 heatsinks, and Asus makes a converter card to adapt a Socket 478 board into a Socket 479 board.

Socket 754—The original socket for AMD's Athlon 64 processors, Socket 754 can also be used for some of the company's new Sempron processors.

Socket 939—AMD's new socket for all AMD64 processors.

Socket 940—The original socket for AMD's Opteron and Athlon 64 FX processors. This has now been made obsolete by Socket 939.

TEC—Thermoelectric converter. A device that uses two dissimilar metals and electric current to produce extreme hot and cold temperatures on either side. TECs are used by overclockers, with the hot side usually water cooled.

TFT—Thin film transistor. The technology used for just about every LCD monitor now.

TIM—Thermal interface material. Put a layer of TIM between a CPU and an HSF and you'll improve the transfer of heat.

Touchscreen—A screen that will respond to being touched. These are usually USB devices that perform the same job as a left click on a mouse.

Transform and lighting—The early stages of the graphics pipeline—the mathematical transformations required to work out where a 3D object is in its world, and the calculations required to work out how it will be lit.

Vertex—A point in 3D space.

Vertex shader—A small program run on a graphics card's GPU to process vertices.

VFD—Vacuum fluorescent display. Looks like an LCD display, but has backlighting too.

Voodoo—Originally, the brand name for 3dfx's graphics chips, but now the name of an enthusiasts' PC brand.

Water block—Part of a water-cooling setup that attaches to the hot parts of your PC, usually in place of heatsinks.

Water loop—A complete water cooling system.

X86—The standard instruction set for PC processors since 1978. Basically, processors can be programmed to do things a number of ways, but to make PCs do the same thing, those programs need to use a single set of instructions. By adhering to or emulating the X86 instruction set, a CPU can ensure compatibility with Windows and all 16-bit and 32-bit PC software.

Xeon—Intel's CPU for servers and workstations. You can run several Xeons in the same machine for multi-processing.

190 > 191

Technical websites and further resources

There are hundreds of technology websites around the world, and it's impossible to list them all in one space. However, I do have a short list of the sites that I check regularly, which I've included below:

www.theinquirer.net—Much like its namesake, The National Enquirer, this website has finely honed the knack of turning rumors into fact. However, it also often gets things right months before anyone else does. It's worth checking this site on a regular basis if you want to keep in touch with what's going on (or what might be going on) in the industry.

www.theregister.co.uk—Originally set up by a team including The Inquirer's Mike Magee, The Register continues to be an excellent source of IT info. It's more professional than The Inquirer, but it's often full of news about servers and the business IT world. It's worth keeping an eye on, though, as it gets some good scoops now and then.

www.bit-tech.net—One of the enthusiasts' favorite sites, Bit-Tech is a fantastic place to pick up advice on modding and customization. If you're working on a project, then post some pictures in the Project Logs section of the forum and you'll get loads of feedback. Bit-Tech also has some great opinion columns and regular news and reviews updates.

www.beyond3d.com—If you want to find out about how 3D graphics cards really work then this is the site to visit. Its editor, Dave Baumann, knows so much about graphics cards that it's difficult to figure out where he stores it all. The discussions on the forums are very technical, but these guys really know their stuff. This is a great site to learn and expand your knowledge from.

www.tomshardware.com—The first technical website to become really mainstream and well known, Tom's Hardware now has a legendary status. Tom has some good bits of opinion on his site, and lots of in-depth technical features and discussions.

www.hexus.net—Started by its editor, David Ross, as a teenage bedroom project, Hexus is now a serious business. There are usually some good scoops on the front page and the forums are always thriving.

www.anandtech.com—Along with Tom's Hardware, Anandtech is the other of the two biggest technical websites. Anandtech is a huge site with great content, and worth checking regularly.

www.gizmodo.com—Although it's mainly a gadget site, Gizmodo also covers a lot of cool stuff in the PC industry, which makes it well worth keeping your eye on.

www.pcperspective.com—This site contains lots of in-depth features that really go into how things work. Unlike many websites, PC Perspective isn't afraid to report the truth of its findings, and its content is very well researched.

www.spodesabode.com—Spode is a cheerful breath of fresh air in an industry that's often clogged up with people who take themselves too seriously. The site doesn't look like much, but it's usually got some good reviews, and it's worth looking at just for Spode's "thumbs up" award logo.

www.hardocp.com—A huge technology website that has incredibly busy forums and lots of in-depth, well-researched technical content.

www.xbitlabs.com—Originally a Russian site, Xbit Labs is now run from the US, although its core labs team is still based in Moscow. Xbit Labs is a great technical resource, with lots of in-depth technical testing and information.

www.mini-itx.com—Dedicated to the world of modding with VIA's Mini-ITX motherboards, this site features hundreds of bizarre PC mods that are great to browse through. It also has a shop for purchasing modding components and Mini-ITX boards.

www.kustompcs.co.uk—A fantastic site for purchasing modding components. KustomPCs has a great record in customer service and a knowledgeable team of staff, not to mention a thriving forum community.

www.custompc.co.uk—Custom PC's website has a great forum community and the magazine's staff regularly contribute as well.

www.austinmodders.com—A friendly and extremely competent team of modders. Their projects range from wooden iPods to PCs in the shape of cocktail glasses that can be fixed to barroom walls.

www.bonzai-mods.com—This store is a modder's paradise. It sells custom-designed mod parts, such as fan grills and reservoirs for cooling systems.